The Team Effectiveness Survey Workbook

Also available from ASQ Quality Press:

Virtual Teams Guidebook for Managers
Herb Dreo, Pat Kunkel, and Thomas Mitchell

Quality Makes Money: How to Involve Every Person on the Payroll in a Complete Quality Process (CQP)
Pat Townsend and Joan Gebhardt

Of Tails and Teams: A Fable for Children and CEOs
H. James Harrington, Ernst & Young, L.L.P.

101 Good Ideas: How to Improve Just About Any Process
Karen Bemowski and Brad Stratton, editors

Team Based Product Development Guidebook
Norman Reilly

Team Fitness: A How-To Manual for Building a Winning Work Team
Meg Hartzler and Jane Henry, Ph.D.

Tools for Virtual Teams: A Team Fitness Companion
Meg Hartzler and Jane Henry, Ph.D.

Lessons from Team Leaders: A Team Fitness Companion
Jane Henry, Ph.D.

Making Change Work: Practical Tools for Overcoming Human Resistance to Change
Brien Palmer

The Path to Profitable Measures: 10 Steps to Feedback That Fuels Performance
Mark W. Morgan

The Quality Improvement Handbook
ASQ Quality Management Division and John E. Bauer, Grace L. Duffy,
and Russell T. Westcott, editors

The Quality Toolbox, Second Edition
Nancy R. Tague

To request a complimentary catalog of ASQ Quality Press publications, call 800-248-1946, or visit our Web site at http://qualitypress.asq.org.

The Team Effectiveness Survey Workbook

Robert W. Bauer and Sandra S. Bauer

ASQ Quality Press
Milwaukee, Wisconsin

American Society for Quality, Quality Press, Milwaukee 53203

© 2006 by American Society for Quality

All rights reserved. Published 2005

Printed in the United States of America

12 11 10 09 08 07 06 05   5 4 3 2 1

Library of Congress Cataloging-in-Publication Data

Bauer, Robert W., 1938–

   The team effectiveness survey workbook / Robert W. Bauer and Sandra S. Bauer.

     p. cm.

   Includes index.

   ISBN-13: 978-0-87389-672-6 (alk. paper)

   1. Teams in the workplace—Evaluation—Handbooks, manuals, etc.

   2. Surveys.   I. Bauer, Sandra S.   II. Title.

   HD66.B388 2005

   658.4′022—dc22

                        2005022406

Publisher: William A. Tony

Acquisitions Editor: Annemieke Hytinen

Project Editor: Paul O'Mara

Production Administrator: Randall Benson

ASQ Mission: The American Society for Quality advances individual, organizational, and community excellence worldwide through learning, quality improvement, and knowledge exchange.

Attention Bookstores, Wholesalers, Schools, and Corporations: ASQ Quality Press books, videotapes, audiotapes, and software are available at quantity discounts with bulk purchases for business, educational, or instructional use. For information, please contact ASQ Quality Press at 800-248-1946, or write to ASQ Quality Press, P.O. Box 3005, Milwaukee, WI 53201-3005.

To place orders or to request a free copy of the ASQ Quality Press Publications Catalog, including ASQ membership information, call 800-248-1946. Visit our Web site at www.asq.org or http://qualitypress.asq.org.

Quality Press
600 N. Plankinton Avenue
Milwaukee, Wisconsin 53203
Call toll free 800-248-1946
Fax 414-272-1734
www.asq.org
http://qualitypress.asq.org
http://standardsgroup.asq.org
E-mail: authors@asq.org

∞ Printed on acid-free paper

Table of Contents

CD-ROM Contents

The following files are available on the CD-ROM accompanying this book. To access them, you will need word processing software such as Microsoft Word. **See page 83 for additional information about the CD-ROM.**

Sample Output Report

File name: Sample Survey Output Report.doc

Sample Questionnaires

File names: Team Implementation Survey.doc
Team Meeting Effectiveness Survey.doc
Team Readiness Survey.doc

Survey Questions

File name: Survey Questions.doc

Survey Support Materials

File names: Electronic Survey Design Template.doc
Mail-In Survey Announcement Letter.doc
Sample Survey Announcement Letter.doc
Sample Survey Code List—version 1.doc
Sample Survey Code List—version 2.doc

Preface

Virtually every type (business, healthcare, education, government, military, and religious) and size of organization is committing substantial resources (money, people, and time) to team-based initiatives. Although there are many different names applied to these teams (Corrective Action Teams, Project Teams, Quality Improvement Teams, and method-specific teams such as Six Sigma, lean, quality function deployment, and strategy deployment teams), their purpose is similar: *Improve organization quality, performance, productivity, and effectiveness*. It is also evident that when resources are properly used, the positive impact on an organization can be extraordinary. Research and the authors' experience have shown that moving toward a more collaborative, mission-focused, team-based environment leads to substantial and long-lasting improvements in an organization's financial performance.

In our experience—more than 60 years of working with organizations to implement a team-based, participative environment—we have found that many, if not most, organizations that undertake initiatives to implement a team environment fail to reach their objectives. There are several reasons why this occurs:

- The organization's culture or climate is not ready for or supportive of a team environment.

- Team members and leaders are not adequately trained.

- Team members and leaders are not adequately supported—this can take many forms, including not being given sufficient time to effectively participate in team activities, lack of needed resources (funds, equipment, facilities), lack of support from management, and so on.

- Team goals and objectives are not clear-cut, obtainable, or integrated with organization goals and objectives.

- Team involvement and success are not recognized.

Often, the reasons why team activities and programs fail are simply not evident to team members, team leaders, and upper management because there is no system in place to measure what is actually occurring. The *Team Effectiveness Survey Workbook* has been developed to help provide invaluable information that allows organizations to:

- Assess readiness to undertake team-based initiatives. If the organization is not ready, the focus should be on initiatives that will correct the situation.

- Assess team effectiveness during the implementation process and undertake corrective action when needed.

- Track changes over time in the implementation of team-based initiatives—these measures can be most useful in team recognition/reward programs and in validating the investment made in the initiative.

In essence, use of the *Workbook* allows you and your organization to follow a medical model approach to the assessment of your team-based initiatives—diagnosis before treatment. Rather than wait until problems become readily apparent and costly, it becomes possible to deal with them at a much earlier time through use of the survey results. It takes you through all of the steps necessary to conduct successful team-based surveys and gives you a wide range of tools to save you time and ensure that the results will be of benefit to you and your organization.

The *Workbook* has been developed for use by internal and external resource persons and consultants who are responsible for team development and implementation activities, as well as team leaders and members involved in team-based initiatives.

We appreciate the time and effort of the Quality Press reviewers, Jackie Creasy, William LaFollette, Joseph J. Pelley, Matt Redmond, and Garry Schultz; and Paul O'Mara, our Project Editor. Their contributions were extremely helpful in making this a better book.

Bob and Sandy Bauer
July 2005

Introduction

The *Team Effectiveness Survey Workbook* has been created to assist you in conducting diagnostic surveys in your organization. This workbook will help you to:

- Develop survey objectives.

- Prepare your survey questionnaire.

- Create a survey code structure for summarizing the results.

- Administer the survey.

- Process the survey results.

- Analyze and feed back the survey results.

The *Workbook* provides detailed assistance in developing your survey questionnaires. Section 2 contains more than 500 different questions, divided into 28 categories to help you create survey questionnaires to meet your specific information needs. In addition, throughout this workbook you will find sample questionnaires, answer sheets, code structures, and so on, along with examples and forms to aid you in constructing a survey. Finally, the *Workbook* includes a Team Effectiveness CD-ROM Toolkit that contains all of the survey questions in their appropriate categories, the sample Team Effectiveness questionnaires, and all of the survey support materials contained in Section 4. You can use the materials on the CD-ROM as needed in your survey efforts.

Note: The term "team" as used in this book is intended to represent all types of teams, including problem-solving groups, cross-functional groups, project teams, corrective action teams, task forces, quality improvement teams, and so on. The term "team program/process" will be used throughout this workbook as a generic name that can be applied to any of these types of teams.

Section 1

The Survey Process

This section takes you step by step through the activities required to have a successful survey effort. We recommend that the steps be completed in sequence for each survey you conduct. Use of these steps will help prevent problems and ensure that you get the desired results from the survey. The steps are:

Developing survey objectives

Creating the survey questionnaire

Survey coding

Survey administration

Survey processing

Analyzing and reporting survey results

DEVELOPING SURVEY OBJECTIVES

There are many occasions when the collection of survey data can be helpful in the implementation of a team program/process. For instance, the survey results can help you to:

- Determine the organization's readiness to undertake the development of a team program/process.

- Collect benchmark information prior to undertaking the creation of teams for use in subsequent assessment efforts.

- Determine the organization's strengths, problem areas, and opportunities for improvement, which can be used to guide team efforts.

- Evaluate the effectiveness of team training.

- Monitor and evaluate team progress and effectiveness.

- Identify areas of the team program/process that need further improvement.

The first step in *any* survey effort should be the development of specific objectives for the survey. Although this may seem obvious, we have frequently seen situations where the objectives were not sufficiently specified, understood, and/or accepted. The survey effort was then seen as a waste of time or a failure.

Please note that it is not sufficient to have a broad, vague objective like "to find out what people think." It is important that the survey objectives specify:

- *Why* the survey is to be undertaken

- *What* the survey will measure

- *Who* will be involved

- *When* the effort will be started and completed

- *How* the results are to be used

A detailed example of an objectives statement for a team readiness survey is shown in Exhibit I.

Also note that in certain situations (generally when you are surveying large numbers of people to assess general perceptions/issues), you may wish to obtain survey data on a random-sample basis. A well planned and constructed random sample provides reliable information with less effort and disruption. Random-sample surveys also tend to raise fewer expectations about what will occur as a result of the survey effort.

When the survey objectives are defined, they can then be used to:

- Obtain the management support needed for the survey.

- Determine the survey questions.

- Create the survey questionnaire.

- Communicate the purpose of the survey to organization members.

- Select survey participants.

- Develop the survey coding structure necessary to ensure appropriate analysis and feedback of results.

If your survey effort is going to be a success, careful planning is essential. You want to make sure that:

- Respondents understand the survey questions.

- The right questions are asked.

- The survey results can be summarized in a meaningful way to provide needed information for management.

- The gathering of irrelevant information is kept to a minimum.

How the survey information will be used should be determined *before* the survey is conducted, not after. To illustrate this point, let's look at a recent survey conducted at a fictional company, Cadbury Enterprises. Cadbury executive management wanted information from quality team participants to determine how well the quality team process was being

Exhibit I

CADBURY ENTERPRISES

Survey Objectives

Organization Readiness Survey

Reason for the Survey: To assess organization readiness to undertake a team approach to our quality improvement efforts.

Survey Objectives

The survey will be conducted to:

- Determine levels of support and commitment for the proposed team approach to the quality improvement effort by each major hierarchical level (non-supervisory members, first-level supervisors, middle managers, top management).

- Determine levels of support and commitment for the proposed team process by each major department.

- Determine level of interest in participating in the team process (facilitators, team leaders, team members).

- Determine potential obstacles to successful implementation of the team process (management receptivity to lower level suggestions, organization climate for innovation and risk taking, perceived concern for members, and so on).

The survey will measure the following:

- Organization climate in terms of:
  - Management's openness to greater employee involvement in decisions affecting their work
  - Management's willingness to listen to employees
  - Encouragement of innovation/new ways of doing things
  - Collaboration vs. competition
  - Management's receptivity to the precepts of the team process
  - Quality of employee/management relations

- Employee perceptions of the importance of quality

- Employee perceptions of the level of collaboration in the organization

- Employee perceptions of their role in the organization

(continued)

- Perceived levels of support and commitment at the different major organization levels and by major functional areas—assess "how supportive am I" and "how supportive are they" (management, non-supervisory employees) of the proposed quality team process

- Level of knowledge/awareness of the proposed quality team process content and requirements

- Willingness to participate in the proposed quality team process

Note: The questionnaire should be limited to the fewest number of questions necessary to meet the objectives and should provide an opportunity for open-ended responses from participants to describe their view of the proposed quality team process.

The following organization members will be involved in the survey:

- Each major hierarchical level, with the exception of directors and vice-presidents, will be surveyed using a random sample.

- *All* directors and vice-presidents will be surveyed.

- Surveys will be conducted in group settings of 40 to 50 people, in the training center.

- Survey administrators will be provided by the Human Resources Department training staff.

Survey Administration Plan

The following dates are proposed to complete the required steps in the survey effort:

June 1	Obtain top management approval of the survey objectives and time frame.
June 15	Select survey participants.
June 30	Review, finalize, and approve survey questionnaire.
July 7	Complete draft of survey questionnaire.
July 10	Announce survey to organization members.
July 17	Schedule survey participants for survey administration.
July 31	Complete survey data collection effort.
August 15	Process survey results and prepare report of findings.
August 21	Review survey report with management and determine future actions.
September 10	Release summary of results to the organization.

(continued)

(continued)

Using the Results

The results of the survey are:

- Summarized by key areas described in the "Survey Objectives" section.
- Reviewed with top and middle management to:
  - –Determine readiness for the quality team process.
  - –Identify obstacles/problems that could impact successful implementation of the quality team process.
  - –Determine actions/strategies for overcoming identified obstacles/problems.
  - –Gain commitment for the quality team process.

implemented in the organization. Members of the quality team steering committee created the survey, conducted it, processed the results, and gave management a summary of results for all respondents.

After reviewing the results, executive management decided to take action to improve the quality team process. They wanted managers from each division to review the results from their individual areas and develop action plans. To assist managers in this activity, executive management wanted to provide each manager with a summary of the survey results from their individual area so that they could feed back the results to participating employees.

The steering committee had not anticipated a request to break down the survey data in this way and did not use a code structure that would allow the results to be sorted by department. As a result, executive management's need for additional breakdowns of the data to support an improvement effort could not be met.

As you can see in the example, better up-front planning and objective setting could have made the survey effort much more useful to the organization. Clearly defined objectives are instrumental in getting the survey effort off to a good start and ensuring that the end results meet the expectations of people throughout the organization.

It is essential that members from all levels of the organization be involved throughout the survey process, including representative team members who have an interest in the survey effort. They can provide useful information and insight that will ensure a successful survey effort. How this involvement takes place will vary from organization to organization.

CREATING THE SURVEY QUESTIONNAIRE

Creating a survey questionnaire can be one of the more difficult and time-consuming steps in the survey process. This becomes apparent when you sit down with a blank piece of paper and try to create just the right questions to get the necessary information from survey participants. Section 2 contains more than 500 questions to help get you started.

The questions in Section 2 all use a 5-point extent scale (a Likert scale) to measure respondents' views. You are not limited to this scale. You may wish to modify the questions to fit another scale or type of response, depending upon your particular needs. Following are examples of some commonly used response scales.

Extent Scale

To what extent are supervisors in this organization receptive to ideas from subordinates?
1. To a very little extent
2. To a little extent
3. To some extent
4. To a great extent
5. To a very great extent

Agree/Disagree Scale (Version 1)

Supervisors in this organization are receptive to ideas from subordinates.
1. Strongly disagree
2. Disagree
3. Undecided
4. Agree
5. Strongly agree

Agree/Disagree Scale (Version 2)

Supervisors in this organization are receptive to ideas from subordinates.
1. Disagree
2. Somewhat disagree
3. Undecided
4. Somewhat agree
5. Agree

Yes/No Scale

Supervisors in this organization are receptive to ideas from subordinates.
1. Yes
2. Don't know
3. No

Questions can also be formulated so that the response options describe alternatives and the respondents must select the description that comes closest to their view of the situation. These are multiple-choice questions. Other questions may require the respondent to supply a numeric value, such as age or length of service. This information can be obtained through the use of a multiple-choice question or by having the respondent supply the actual number on the answer sheet.

A *critical factor* in evaluating what type of scale to use is *your capability to process the results*. If you intend to process the results manually, you can use any of the response options. If you intend to process the results by computer, the software program must accommodate both your response choices and the number of response options you provide.

Several guidelines to assist you in creating your survey questionnaire follow:

- Ask only the questions that support your survey objectives. Do not include questions that would generate information that would just "be nice to know" or information you do not need to meet your objectives. This will help keep your questionnaire focused and manageable in length.

- Use as few different scales as possible. Using many different scales tends to be confusing to survey participants, complicates the task of survey layout, and can make the job of interpreting results more difficult.

- Avoid questions that appear to have a positive or negative bias. The credibility of the survey may be severely undermined if participants think the survey has been created to support a particular (management's) point of view.

- When laying out the survey, leave lots of white space in the questionnaire so that it is easy to read. A crowded questionnaire can be confusing to the respondent.

- Do not ask trick questions, or questions that may be perceived to have a "right" or "wrong" answer. You do not want survey participants spending time guessing what the answer should be rather than answering candidly.

- Make sure the survey instructions are clearly written. This is especially critical when the survey is to be conducted by mail or when a survey administrator will not be present to explain the survey procedures and answer questions.

- We recommend that you pre-test the survey to ensure that the instructions and questions will be clearly understood by survey participants. Pre-testing with a sample survey group or with people not involved in the creation of the survey helps detect problems that, if left unresolved, will adversely impact the reliability of the results.

- When developing your survey questions, have each question focus on the one discrete variable that you want to measure. If you include more than one variable in a single question, respondents will be confused as to what the question is asking. This also poses problems in data analysis because you cannot be sure which variable was being addressed by the respondent.

- Avoid asking questions about a subject if the participants have no information or experience upon which to formulate an accurate response.

- Demographic questions (age, sex, race, and so forth) should be used sparingly and with great care. Experience has shown that increasing the number of demographic questions can be threatening to survey participants and can result in less candid responses.

Regardless of the type of survey, consider the use of an "additional comments" page. This allows respondents to provide you with descriptive, open-ended information related to the areas measured by the survey. This information can be very useful in identifying important, specific issues not directly addressed in the scaled survey questions. Section 2 provides examples of questions requiring a narrative response.

Using a separate answer sheet may facilitate the processing of survey results. This is also more economical because the questionnaires are reusable. Having respondents record their answers on the questionnaire may be necessary, however, when a variety of question types—for example, checklists, narrative responses, and multiple choice—are needed to gather the necessary information and to accommodate different response scales.

Most important of all, the questions selected should be carefully related to the predetermined survey objectives. The questions from the sample Team Readiness Survey in Section 3 provide an example of how this can be accomplished. If you carefully examine the included questions, you will see that they are related to the specific objectives described in Exhibit I in this section.

SURVEY CODING

If you need to display your survey results in a variety of ways (by department, function, hierarchical level, team, and so forth), you must develop a code structure to accommodate the required output reports. This code structure is then used by all survey participants to ensure that their survey answers can be summarized into designated survey reports.

The complexity of the survey code structure is directly related to the level of analysis required. If you are conducting a small survey and only want to sort the results into a limited number of survey output reports, the code structure can be very simple. If, on the other hand, you are conducting a large survey across several sites and need many reports from the survey results, the code structure may become much more complex.

A general rule to follow in developing a survey code structure is to make it sufficiently detailed to cover all anticipated output reports required when analyzing the survey results. *If the needed reports to be processed from the survey data have not been identified and coded, they can't be retrieved or summarized after the fact.*

The remainder of this section deals with the development of sample code structures. The examples are sufficiently detailed to allow you to effectively code all but the most complex, large-scale surveys.

As a general guideline, a well-developed survey code structure will:

- Allow you to identify relevant respondent information in order to prepare required survey output reports.

- Provide the necessary structure to process the survey results.

- Provide sufficient respondent anonymity to ensure individual responses cannot be identified, if this is considered important.

A code number is a series of digits linked to specific characteristics of the individuals being surveyed. The characteristics could include the respondent's:

- Organization (site) location

- Department/unit

- Supervisor

- Hierarchical level (non-supervisory, hourly/salaried, exempt/non-exempt, middle manager, executive-level manager)

- Functional area (nature of work performed—sales, finance, production, engineering)

- Demographic data (age, length of service, education level)

- Work shift

We have found that describing how to assign the survey code numbers tends to be more complicated than actually *doing* the coding. Understanding the relationship of the assigned numbers to their use in processing helps ease the coding task and also makes the need for accuracy in code assignment more obvious.

The first step in the survey coding process is to determine how you want to sort the survey results. Your survey objectives will help you make the proper decisions. You want to be able to sort the survey data to support your information requirements. Carefully evaluate what cuts of data will be necessary to provide the information you need.

For each different cut of the survey results required, you will need a code digit or set of digits to determine what responses need to be combined to produce desired output reports.

To illustrate the survey coding process, we will use the Cadbury Enterprises Organization Readiness Survey (described in Exhibit I) as an example. Based on the objectives, let us assume that the survey results will be analyzed and reported back to management using the following:

- By site location

- By respondent's functional designation/area

- By department within each site

- By hierarchical level within each site

To develop an accurate, complete code structure, each of these elements must be determined and assigned a number that is then used by the survey participants on their survey answer sheets.

Let us further assume that we will use a six-digit code structure to capture the required information and that Cadbury Enterprises has the following organization structure:

- There are fewer than 10 site locations in Cadbury Enterprises.

- There are 10 major functional designations/areas within the company.

- There are fewer than 100 departments at each site.

- There are 10 hierarchical levels at each site.

- There are three shift designations.

Given this information, we can establish a basic framework for our six-digit code structure as follows:

Digit	Used to identify
[1]	Site
[2]	Major function
[3]	Department
[4]	Department
[5]	Hierarchical level
[6]	Shift

With this framework established, we can begin to develop the detailed code structure. In order to do this accurately and efficiently, you will need up-to-date organization charts, personnel rosters, manning tables, and so forth to be able to identify survey participants and assign them proper codes.

Let us now assume that Cadbury Enterprises has three manufacturing plants and a corporate headquarters. We can assign the site codes as follows:

Digit no. [1]	Used to identify: Site
Code no.	**Site location**
[1]	Ann Arbor assembly
[2]	Ann Arbor components
[3]	Taylor machine shop
[4]	Corporate headquarters

Using Cadbury Enterprises' organization charts, we can identify and code the major functions (digit 2). This might appear as follows:

Digit no. [2]	Used to identify: Major function
Code no.	**Major function**
[0]	Maintenance
[1]	Engineering
[2]	Manufacturing
[3]	Assembly
[4]	Distribution
[5]	Quality assurance
[6]	Sales and marketing
[7]	Finance and administration
[8]	Human resources
[9]	Information technology

The next two digits in Cadbury Enterprises' code structure (digits 3 and 4) are used to identify individual departments. You have some options to consider when assigning these codes. For example, you might code a department by using an alphabetic listing of all departments and assigning the codes in numeric sequence to the alphabetic list:

Digit no. [3, 4]	Used to identify: Department
Code no.	**Department**
[01]	Accounting
[02]	Advertising
[03]	Assembly area #1
[04]	Assembly area #2
⇓	⇓

Or, if departments are already coded numerically for company purposes, you may choose to assign department survey codes in the same sequence:

Digit no. [3, 4]	Used to identify: Department
Code no.	**Department**
[01]	1100 Laboratory
[02]	1110 Credit
[03]	1120 Product administration
[04]	1130 Warehouse
⇓	⇓

Another option would be to assign department codes based on the way they appear in the organization chart:

Digit no. [3, 4]	Used to identify: Department
Code no. 70–79	**Finance**
[71]	Credit
[72]	General accounting
[73]	Cost analysis
[74]	Internal audit
⇓	⇓

Please note that department codes may be repeated across different sites. In fact, if you are careful to ensure that the codes are consistent across individual sites, you can consolidate like departments using these codes (assuming your method of processing results will accommodate it).

If, for example, the purchasing departments in each site carried department code 75 and you had the computer software capability to summarize survey results by requesting a consolidation of all survey respondents using 75 in the third and fourth digits, you would obtain the summarized results for *all* purchasing department respondents across all sites.

The fifth digit in Cadbury Enterprises' code structure is used to identify the survey respondent's hierarchical level. This digit might be coded as follows:

Digit no. [5]	Used to identify: Hierarchical level
Code no.	Hierarchical level
[1]	Non-supervisory, hourly
[2]	Non-supervisory, salaried
[3]	First-line supervisors
[4]	Middle managers
[5]	Directors
[6]	Vice-presidents/executive management

The final code number to be assigned (the sixth digit) is that of shift level:

Digit no. [6]	Used to identify: Shift
Code no.	Shift
[1]	First shift
[2]	Second shift
[3]	Third shift

Once the complete code structure has been developed, review it with the key people who have responsibility for the team process to ensure that the survey results can be presented in a way that meets their needs as well as those of the rest of management.

There is one other critical consideration when developing a survey code structure—determining how survey respondents will know what code number to use when taking the survey.

On the surface this may seem like a simple issue, but it really is not, and again, you have some choices to make relating to survey accuracy, ease of coding, and creating a sense of anonymity on the part of the survey respondents.

For example, if you want the survey results to be as accurate as possible, you should determine the code number for every survey participant *prior* to survey administration and give each respondent his or her assigned code number during survey administration (on-site group administration, mail, or electronically). To do this, however, requires a great deal of effort in developing the code list and may threaten the participant's sense of anonymity when he or she is given a specific code number to use.

Another option is to let the survey participants determine their own code numbers to use, based on charts you design (on flip chart pages or overhead transparencies in group administration, or a coding instruction sheet in mail and electronic surveys) and present these to them during survey administration. These sheets would be similar to the ones created for your own use in determining the code structure. This is a less time-consuming approach and usually less threatening to the survey participants, but the chance of miscoding increases (through misunderstanding or willful errors by survey participants).

This issue should be considered carefully and resolved well in advance of survey administration.

A second example of how to develop a code structure follows. In this example, the code structure will be used in a survey designed to assess how well the team process is being implemented. Some of the assumptions underlying the development of the code structure are:

Site where respondents work	Fewer than 10 sites
Teams	More than 99 teams
Respondents' functional areas	Fewer than 10 functions
Hierarchical levels of respondents	Fewer than 10 levels

Digit	Used to identify
[1]	Site
[2]	Team number 1
[3]	Team number 2
[4]	Team number 3
[5]	Respondent's functional area
[6]	Hierarchical level

In our example, the first digit of the code structure indicates the site where the survey respondent works:

Digit no. [1]	Used to identify: Site
Code no.	Site location
[1]	Ann Arbor assembly
[2]	Ann Arbor components
[3]	Taylor machine shop
[4]	Corporate headquarters

The next three digits (2, 3, and 4) are used together to give us enough digits to designate each team in the major locations. The use of the team code allows you to prepare a summary of the results for each team. Prior to coding, create a list of all the teams participating in the survey. From this list, you will gain some idea about how many code numbers will be required in each location (site and department within site).

When assigning code numbers to the teams, the simplest method is to use some form of sequential numbering system. Under this system, fewer errors tend to crop up when you develop instructions as to which sets of data are to be combined for special data summaries. For example, a summary of a large number of teams in the Automotive Products area may be required. If all the teams in this area were coded in the 100 series, instructions for survey processing would be greatly simplified.

For example: Combine all teams using a [1] as the second digit for the creation of a survey output report. Title this output report "Automotive Products Teams."

One difficulty with sequential numbering is that if you omit a group at first and then correct the omission, your numbering becomes mixed rather than sequential. This potential problem can be alleviated by creating a list of all teams before you begin to assign the actual code numbers, and by *reserving enough extra numbers* in each sequence to accommodate additions.

For our example, the team coding of the Automotive Products area is:

Digit no. [2, 3, 4]	Used to identify: Team leader codes
Code nos. 100–199	Team leaders—Automotive Products
[1] [0] [0]	John Adams
[1] [0] [2]	Bill Greenwood
[1] [0] [4]	Sara Jones
[1] [0] [6]	Margaret Wells
[1] [0] [8]	John Wilson
⇓	⇓
[1] [9] [9]	Valerie Noyes

The fifth digit in the code number identifies the functional area in which the respondent works.

Digit no. [5]	Used to identify: Functional area
Code no.	Functional area
[0]	Maintenance
[1]	Engineering
[2]	Manufacturing
[3]	Assembly
[4]	Distribution
[5]	Quality assurance

The sixth digit in the code number identifies the hierarchical level of the respondent.

Digit no. [6]	Used to identify: Hierarchical level
Code no.	Hierarchical level
[1]	Non-supervisory, hourly
[2]	Non-supervisory, salaried
[3]	First-line supervisors
[4]	Middle managers
[5]	Directors
[6]	Vice-presidents/executive management

The information provided thus far gives you two fairly complex examples of how you can set up a code structure. An example of a less complex code structure, using only four digits, is:

Digit	Used to identify
[1]	Plant
[2]	Hierarchical level
[3]	Functional area
[4]	Length of employee service

In any case, the code structure provides the ability to summarize survey results so that you obtain the specific information required to meet your survey objectives. Take great care in planning the code structure prior to administering the survey to ensure that you will obtain the information needed to prepare the required survey output reports.

SURVEY ADMINISTRATION

The degree of effort required to effectively administer a survey will vary greatly depending upon several factors, including:

- Number of people to be surveyed

- Location of survey participants

- Complexity of the code structure and survey instructions

- Determination of how the survey data will be obtained (group administration, by mail, electronically, or a combination of methods)

- Need for confidentiality and anonymity of respondents

- Complexity and length of the survey questionnaire

- Survey participants who have difficulty reading/writing

If the survey data are collected using group administration, determine the:

- Number of survey administration sessions to be held

- Number of survey participants per session

For large, complex surveys, we generally recommend that survey data be collected using group administration, supported by the use of mail-in surveys for small, outlying locations, and for people who are traveling or on vacation/leave. Group administration is efficient and more accurate (the survey requirements can be carefully explained and participant questions answered) and will usually yield a higher participation rate than other data collection methods. Electronic data collection methods are discussed later in this section.

The following pages describe survey administration requirements for a large, complex survey effort. Many of the requirements apply regardless of the size of the survey. They include:

- Preparing for the survey

- Arranging for the physical space required to seat the groups of survey respondents

- Coordinating time schedules for the groups

- Arranging for survey materials to be available at the proper time

- Administering the survey to groups of survey respondents

- Making arrangements for surveys to be conducted by mail

Preparing for the Survey

The final decision to conduct a survey is often made at the upper levels of an organization with the involvement and commitment of the managers who will be affected.

Orientation sessions should be conducted by key persons responsible for the survey to keep managers/supervisors fully informed of *what* needs to be accomplished and *why*. This information-sharing plays a crucial part in gaining the cooperation needed to schedule personnel to take the survey. Workloads may need to be rearranged and proper coverage planned for as employees take time from their jobs to complete the survey. Work schedules may be such that survey administration needs to take place on an overtime basis for some employees. Often, the sharing of accurate information regarding the survey process encourages cooperation from all those affected.

Two to three weeks before the survey, the head of the organization or unit should inform all involved employees of the event. This may be handled through a letter, the company newspaper, special memos on the bulletin board, e-mail, intranet/Internet, or any other avenue normally used to deliver important information to organization members. Any such message should cover:

- The reasons for conducting the survey

- How survey results will be used

- An explanation of how employee anonymity will be maintained, if appropriate

In the message, employees who will be participating should be encouraged to be open and honest in their responses. In addition, this general message should express appreciation for employees' cooperation. A sample letter to survey participants is included in Section 4.

Space Requirements

In arranging for space, the following requirements need to be met:

1. The space must be large enough to comfortably accommodate the group being surveyed.

2. Desks or tables should be supplied so that respondents do not have to write on their laps. Chairs should be spaced far enough apart to permit some privacy.

3. Good lighting and ventilation are important.

4. The area should be free from interruptions. Cafeterias are bad locations around lunch or break times. Ringing phones and the bells and whistles used in some organizations to signal the end of a shift or lunch hours are very distracting.

5. A blackboard or flip chart is helpful for use in describing the survey code structure, survey instructions, and so forth.

Long tables in large, quiet rooms are ideal.

If space is very limited, you may wish to ask persons with private offices to come to the survey administration room to listen to the instruction part of the session. Then, ask them to return to their own offices to fill out the survey and return the materials when they are finished. The drawback with this approach is that people tend to be drawn into tasks other than the survey. They are often delayed in filling out the survey, and their train of thought tends to get interrupted.

Scheduling

Respondents can generally complete a survey of 50 questions or less in half an hour, including written comments. Occasionally, some people will take longer. No time limits should be set. Instructions to the group will usually require 10–15 minutes, including time for answering questions. It is best to schedule groups no closer than one hour apart.

Check your tentative survey administration schedule with the supervisors far enough in advance so that required changes may be handled smoothly. If possible, arrange for a makeup survey day to accommodate people on vacation, on sick leave, or away on business travel. In very large organizations this may involve a fair number of people. Scheduling far enough in advance helps to minimize the number of people involved in such time conflicts.

A Special Circumstance

If there are any persons who have difficulty reading or writing, arrange in advance for a reader, or perhaps a translator, to assist. Offering the assistance of a reader "just in case someone has forgotten their glasses" may also, at times, encourage people with limited reading ability to participate.

Special care should be taken in the selection of readers because these individuals may be required to answer questions about the survey, yet avoid prejudicing respondents' answers. Use separate facilities for this procedure if possible. In some cases, family members might assist a respondent (at home, overnight) who would otherwise be unable to participate. This may sound extreme, but the payoff can be noticeable when an organization extends itself to make sure everyone has an opportunity for input.

Materials

To complete the survey, each respondent must have a survey questionnaire and answer sheet (if used).

A pencil with a good eraser will be needed for each member of the survey group. Bring extras, as pencils seem to disappear easily. We strongly recommend having a pencil sharpener available. Using pencils rather than pens makes changing answers easier and neater.

A box, or an envelope that can be sealed, into which respondents may deposit their own answer sheets helps strengthen the sense of confidentiality.

It is surprising how making coffee, tea, or soft drinks available during the survey relaxes the atmosphere. While this is certainly not a requirement, do think of the positive effect this bit of consideration has on employees' willingness to cooperate.

Survey Administration Day(s)

Arrive early at the survey site. Check the seating arrangements. Participants should have adequate space so that their responses cannot be observed against their will. They may not realize the desire for privacy until after the orientation is given, so it is up to the survey administrator to see that participants are comfortably spaced around the room.

Make sure you have all the materials required. Place a set of survey materials—including the survey questionnaire, written comments page, answer sheet (if used), and a pencil—at the seating place of each respondent.

Be sure a box or envelope is available to receive the respondents' completed surveys/answer sheets at the end of the session.

If a participant must leave before completing the survey, due to illness or an emergency work call, destroy the partially completed survey. Ask the participant to arrange to attend another session to complete the survey.

When all participants have arrived, begin the orientation. Remember, the orientation will set the tone of the survey session.

1. *Explain the purpose of the survey.* Use your survey objectives to clearly explain the intended purpose of the survey.

2. *Describe how results will be used.* Tell participants how the survey results will be analyzed and what they might expect as the outcome of their participation in the survey.

3. *Describe the confidential nature of the survey, if appropriate.* No names are to be placed on the answer sheets. Only summaries of data will be compiled and analyzed.

4. *Request straightforward answers.* There are no right or wrong answers. The most useful answers are those that accurately describe the respondent's viewpoint.

5. *There are no time limits.* Respondents should take enough time to read each question carefully and answer thoughtfully. When finished, they should deposit the answer sheet in the designated box or envelope and leave.

6. *Stress individual effort.* This is not a group or team task. Each individual respondent's views are important.

7. *Read the instructions on the survey questionnaire.* Take time to make sure the instructions are clear. Carefully define the terms in the survey that have a specific meaning, such as who is to be considered when the term "team leader" occurs.

8. *Encourage questions.* Answer questions as honestly as you can. Keep your answers on a positive note. Don't become angry or get involved in a debate.

9. *Say "thank you."* Express appreciation for the group's cooperation in this very important task.

Mail-In Surveys

If you have survey participants at offsite locations, a mail-in survey may be the only feasible method of including them in the survey. If you choose to conduct a mail-in survey, there are several key points to consider:

- Typically only 30–50 percent of the persons who receive the survey by mail respond. If you are taking a random-sample survey, this must be taken into account to obtain an adequate sample size.

- Mail-in surveys take more time—surveys are mailed out, time is required for the participant to complete the survey, and time must be allotted for the survey to be returned by mail. This situation is aggravated if the participant is traveling extensively. Questions to be resolved include:

  –Can surveys be mailed to and collected from a centralized, outlying location?

  –Would response level be improved if the survey were sent directly to the participant's home?

  –What kind of follow-up efforts can be used to encourage participation and prompt return of survey answer sheets (memos, phone calls, e-mail, and so forth)?

  –What provisions are there for business reply envelopes and prepaid postage so that returns may be made easily by mail?

- Surveys should be mailed out well in advance of the on-site survey administration to ensure that survey processing is not delayed for late mail-in surveys.

- Mail-in surveys require detailed instructions to ensure that they are filled out correctly and returned promptly. Sample mail survey instructions are contained in Section 4.

Electronic Survey Data Collection

With the rapid growth of electronic connectivity, intranet and Internet access, and information-sharing capability, there is a greatly increased interest in collecting survey data electronically. Many organizations are now routinely gathering survey data online, and some are achieving very high participation rates in their survey efforts. If you are in this category, the survey coding and data collection methodology will need to be adapted to your particular system.

Three major requirements need to be met when using an electronic data collection approach:

- You need to be certain that all survey participants have access to and understand how to use the electronic survey data collection system. If this is not the case, some potential participants will be excluded from the survey effort, which may lead to biased survey results. In addition, it is likely that the excluded folks will have a strong, negative reaction to being left out.

- Survey participants must trust the data collection system. If they don't, the survey results will likely be biased or participation will be negatively impacted.

- A clear explanation of the survey effort and how to use the electronic survey data collection system must be provided to all potential survey participants in advance. The issue of confidentiality needs to be clearly defined. If this does not occur, it will undoubtedly have a negative impact on the data collection effort.

If you have the budget and an IT department that has the development capability, you may decide to build your own electronic survey data collection system. If not, you may decide to choose an outside vendor to electronically collect your survey data. Some organizations that can assist you in your survey efforts are listed at the end of this section.

SURVEY PROCESSING

There are several options to consider about handling your survey processing requirements. These include:

- Use of a computer spreadsheet software program such as Microsoft Excel and/or a statistical software program such as SPSS.

- Development of your own survey processing software program.

- Purchase of a survey processing software program.

- Use of a service bureau or consulting firm to process your survey results.

Each of these options is discussed briefly below.

Use of Electronic Spreadsheets or Statistical Software

If you have experience using a spreadsheet or statistical software program, you may be able to use the program to process your survey results. It will require a thorough understanding of the program's capabilities and limitations and will likely take some creative experimentation and development time on your part. Microsoft Excel will likely be your spreadsheet choice. If you intend to do some basic statistical analysis (response distributions, correlations, cross-tabs, factor analysis, regressions, and so forth), a statistical software program, such as SPSS or MINITAB, may be best for your needs.

If you already have (or have access to) one of these programs, you may be able to save some time and money using this approach. Remember, however, that some of these packages are not specifically designed to process surveys, in which case they likely will not meet all of your survey processing requirements (ease of data entry, usable report formats, generating breakdowns of the data, and so forth).

Develop Your Own Survey Processing Software Program

If you have sufficient time and money and you will be processing many surveys, you may want to have your IT department develop your own software program to process your surveys. If your organization is already conducting surveys, you may be able to gain access to an internally developed program that meets your requirements.

The major advantage of this approach is that the software system can be designed to meet *your* specific requirements. The disadvantages of this approach include the time and cost involved in developing the system (both of which can be substantial) and the distinct possibility that the system won't live up to expectations when (or, in some cases, if) it is completed.

If you choose to go this route, make sure you spend adequate time up front defining the system requirements from input to final output. This reduces the risk that the system won't meet your needs after an investment of considerable resources.

Purchase a Computer Survey Software Program

If you will be conducting several surveys, you may decide the best approach is to acquire a survey software program. These programs have become increasingly flexible and sophisticated. The drawback to this approach is that some of these programs can be complicated and difficult to use, requiring a relatively high level of computer expertise. The plus side is the immediate availability of a system in-house.

Outside Survey Processing

If you are conducting large, complex surveys, or if you do not have the in-house capability to process survey results, you may want to have your surveys processed by an outside firm. Several service bureaus and consulting firms provide this kind of service.

See Section 4 for a list of resources to help you in processing your survey.

ANALYZING AND REPORTING SURVEY RESULTS

When deciding how to analyze and report survey results, there are several key guidelines to keep in mind:

- Make sure the analysis and resulting report(s) are related to and consistent with the survey objectives.

- Understand your audience's requirements and limitations. *Do not*:
  – Overwhelm them with details (stick to the important points)
  – Assume they are as knowledgeable as you are about the survey and its meaning/implications

- Do not go beyond what is shown in the data. Avoid conclusions that can't be adequately supported.

- Confidentiality and anonymity, if promised, must be maintained at all costs.

Because of the wide range of questionnaire types and variations in reporting requirements, it is not possible to cover the full range of analysis and report options in this workbook. The rest of this section, however, contains some of the more common ways of analyzing and reporting survey results.

Exhibit II contains a sample printout of survey results based on the Team Readiness Survey questionnaire in Section 3. To simplify the illustrative ways of analyzing and reporting survey results, please note that:

- The survey results report contained in Exhibit II represents only one department from one site location in Cadbury Enterprises—a real survey would generate many more reports for other departments and sites, as well as other types of organization summaries.

- Any written report that contains an analysis of the survey results should:
  – Be technically sound
  – Be clear, concise, and readily understood by those who may be unfamiliar with survey concepts and techniques
  – Focus on significant findings
  – Summarize results in such a way that significant points can be quickly grasped
  – Present a balanced picture by covering strengths as well as problem areas
  – Highlight areas requiring improvement

Exhibit II

CADBURY ENTERPRISES—ANN ARBOR ENGINEERING GROUP

Team Readiness Survey Results

Q#	Question	No. of resp.	Mean score	% Resp. 1–2	% Resp. 4–5	Diff. from All Resp.
1.	To what extent does Cadbury Enterprises have a real interest in the welfare and satisfaction of those who work here?	85	3.09	26.6	40.0	–0.03
2.	To what extent do you look forward to coming to work each day?	83	2.97	30.0	30.1	–0.15
3.	To what extent do you understand how your job fits in with other work going on at Cadbury Enterprises?	85	3.90	16.7	**63.3**	**+0.25**
4.	To what extent are the equipment and resources you work with adequate, efficient, and well maintained?	84	3.43	16.7	43.3	**+0.36**
5.	To what extent are your skills and abilities being used?	85	2.97	26.7	26.7	–0.11
6.	To what extent are you satisfied with your job?	85	3.47	19.6	**52.0**	+0.22
7.	To what extent does Cadbury Enterprises provide sufficient training for its employees?	85	2.60	**50.2**	16.3	–0.24
8.	To what extent is Cadbury Enterprises concerned about product/ service quality?	85	3.65	13.5	**55.6**	**+0.26**
9.	To what extent is there an emphasis on teamwork at Cadbury Enterprises?	84	2.54	**51.3**	16.7	–0.23
10.	To what extent can employees influence issues affecting the quality of their work life?	85	**2.43**	**53.5**	12.6	**–0.30**
11.	To what extent *are* non-supervisory employees at Cadbury Enterprises involved in solving work-related problems?	85	2.76	46.7	31.4	–0.11

(continued)

Q#	Question	No. of resp.	Mean score	% Resp. 1–2	% Resp. 4–5	Diff. from All Resp.
12.	To what extent *should* non-supervisory employees be involved in solving work-related problems?	85	3.96	13.0	**69.8**	+0.08
13.	To what extent is the work climate or culture of Cadbury Enterprises likely to support team activities?	85	3.11	26.7	39.2	−0.01
14.	To what extent do different departments work together effectively to solve cross-departmental problems?	84	2.64	49.4	17.1	−0.21
15.	To what extent does management stress product/service quality over quantity at Cadbury Enterprises?	85	3.26	23.3	46.8	+0.05
16.	Communication is a two-way street: To what extent does management listen as well as talk?	85	3.33	21.0	48.2	+0.02
17.	To what extent would you like to see a team approach to improve product/service quality at Cadbury Enterprises?	84	3.89	6.6	**65.7**	+0.21
18.	To what extent is top management likely to support team activities at Cadbury Enterprises?	85	3.42	18.7	43.3	−0.11
19.	To what extent is your supervisor willing to allow you to participate in team activities?	85	3.76	12.2	**62.0**	+0.08
20.	To what extent is your supervisor supportive of the team concept?	85	3.65	13.8	**58.1**	−0.04
21.	To what extent would you like to take a leadership role in team activities?	85	3.79	11.8	**60.5**	+0.19
22.	To what extent do you understand how team activities can benefit Cadbury Enterprises?	84	**4.02**	13.3	**70.3**	+0.12
23.	To what extent do you think team activities will be a success at Cadbury Enterprises?	85	3.56	12.8	**52.1**	+0.02
24.	To what extent has the proposed team activity concept for Cadbury Enterprises been adequately communicated to you?	83	3.23	16.7	43.3	−0.11

Sample Analysis of Survey Results

If we at Bauer & Associates were analyzing the survey results contained in Exhibit II, we would look for the following:

Potential Strengths

- 50 percent or more of the participants responding 4–5
- Scores of 4.00 or higher
- 0.25 points higher than the All Respondents (total organization) score

Potential Problem Areas

- 50 percent or more of the participants responding 1–2
- Scores of 2.50 or lower
- 0.25 points lower than the All Respondents score

The questions where responses met these criteria appear in bold type in Exhibit II and would normally be the primary focus of the analysis and survey results report. It should be noted, however, that questions that show lower percentages of unfavorable responses should not be ignored—the question always should be, "Can we as an organization afford to live with that percentage of organization members responding unfavorably?" If not, then corrective action should be undertaken.

Please also note that the survey results report is only the starting point. It can be very useful in getting a focus on issues that are affecting the team process. Ultimate success comes from using the results to help identify and resolve key organization issues and opportunities for improvement.

Section 2

Survey Questions

This section contains more than 500 questions placed into 28 subject categories for use in creating survey questionnaires to assess your organization's team program/process—from the concept stage through implementation and measurement of results. Based on the *subject* and *object* of each question and the categories we have created, some questions apply to more than one category. For example, the first question in Category 1—Accountability ("To what extent does this organization respond to employee concerns about quality?") also relates to Category 18—Quality. If you look in Category 18, you will see that this question is also included in that category.

When the questions have been placed in multiple categories, a cross-reference is given to the other categories in which the question appears. Cross-references appear after the question, enclosed in brackets [ ].

Note: Because there are many different types of teams, "_____ team(s)" is used in the question lists. If you have a specific designation or name for teams in your organization, it would be inserted into the questions.

Index of Question Categories

	Question category	Page
1	Accountability	28
2	Bureaucracy	29
3	Communications	29
4	Coordination	30
5	Decision Making	31
6	Demographics	32
7	Facilitation	34
8	Innovation and Creativity	35
9	Management	36
10	Meeting Practices	37
11	Member Role	38

	Question category	Page
12	Organization Conditions	39
13	Organization Readiness	39
14	Participation	40
15	Planning	41
16	Problem Solving	42
17	Process Skills	44
18	Quality	45
19	Recording	47
20	Results	47
21	Review	49
22	Rewards	49
23	Supervision	50
24	Team Functioning	51
25	Team Leadership	53
26	Team Member Interaction	54
27	Training	55
28	Written Comment Questions	56

QUESTIONS BY CATEGORY

1—Accountability

1-1 To what extent does this organization respond to employee concerns about quality? [18]

1-2 To what extent does this organization respond to customer concerns about quality? [18]

1-3 To what extent are people in this organization held accountable for producing quality work? [18]

1-4 To what extent are you held accountable for producing quality work? [18]

1-5 To what extent does your team leader maintain high standards of performance? [25]

1-6 To what extent do persons in your team maintain high standards of performance? [26]

1-7 To what extent does your supervisor maintain high standards of performance? [23]

1-8 To what extent does your supervisor hold you accountable for achieving high, but realistic, performance goals? [23]

1-9 To what extent do you know the quality standards or requirements of your job? [9, 13, 18]

1-10 To what extent does this organization attempt to correct the cause of quality problems? [18]

1-11 To what extent does this organization try to improve quality? [18]

1-12 To what extent are _____ team members held accountable to produce results?

1-13 To what extent have clear, specific performance goals been established for your job? [12]

1-14 To what extent does your supervisor expect you to be responsible for correcting your own errors?

2—Bureaucracy

2-1 To what extent is the job you have now free from rules and regulations that no one seems to be able to explain?

2-2 To what extent is overlap or duplication in the work you do kept to a minimum?

2-3 To what extent is there a logical and efficient flow of the work done by this department or unit?

2-4 To what extent is the job you have now free from a lot of "red tape" in getting things done?

2-5 To what extent do you understand how your job fits in with other work going on in this organization? [12]

2-6 To what extent are your work activities sensibly organized?

2-7 To what extent does your supervisor eliminate overlapping responsibilities?

2-8 To what extent does your supervisor eliminate unnecessary activities?

2-9 To what extent does your supervisor arrange work for the most effective handling assignments?

2-10 To what extent are you as productive as you could be? [20]

2-11 To what extent do the company's policies and procedures support the _____ team process?

2-12 To what extent has the amount of bureaucracy and red tape in the team process been kept to a minimum?

2-13 To what extent are the organization's policies and procedures supportive of employee involvement? [13, 14]

3—Communications

3-1 To what extent are you better able to communicate with management now than in the past? [20]

3-2 To what extent do you receive adequate information about team activities from across the organization?

3-3 To what extent are team successes recognized in the organization? [20, 22]

3-4 To what extent do all sides of an issue get discussed? [10, 17]

3-5 To what extent are members willing to express their *real* feelings about problems or issues?

3-6 To what extent are you satisfied with the information you receive about the organization?

3-7   To what extent is there effective communication among your team members?

3-8   To what extent does the organization generally try to keep employees well informed?

3-9   Communication is a two-way street: To what extent does management listen as well as talk?

3-10 To what extent does the organization generally try to follow up on service by talking to customers?

3-11 To what extent are you kept informed about the results of jobs you have worked on in the past?

3-12 To what extent does management not keep you in the dark about things you need to know? [16]

3-13 To what extent is your supervisor free with praise for work that is of high quality? [22, 23]

3-14 To what extent does management communicate the reasons for important decisions to your team? [5]

3-15 To what extent does your supervisor consult subordinates before making a decision that may affect their work? [5, 23]

3-16 To what extent have successful teams been identified as role models for the rest of the organization? [20, 22]

3-17 To what extent have managers who support _____ teams been identified as role models for the rest of the organization? [20, 23]

3-18 To what extent has the experience gained by individual teams been shared with all other teams to improve the entire process? [20]

3-19 To what extent have the results achieved by teams been adequately documented and communicated? [20]

3-20 To what extent has the proposed _____ team process at _____ been adequately communicated? [13]

3-21 To what extent do you get adequate feedback about how you are doing your job?

3-22 To what extent is information about the level of quality performance communicated within your organization?

3-23 To what extent are you given the information you need to know to do your job in the best possible way? [23]

3-24 To what extent is the downward flow of information in this organization adequate? [12]

3-25 To what extent is management free with praise for work done by your team that is of high quality?

4—Coordination

4-1 To what extent do different units/departments/teams plan together and coordinate their efforts? [15]

4-2 To what extent are problems between teams and the formal organization resolved at the level where they appear, through mutual effort and understanding?

4-3 To what extent are _____ teams used to solve problems that affect more than one department?

4-4 To what extent do supervisors and managers actively encourage cross-department cooperation and coordination?

4-5 To what extent are the relationships between your department and other departments cooperative?

4-6 To what extent is your team leader effective in coordinating the work of your team?

4-7 To what extent does the work of your team require sharing knowledge and information with a variety of other teams or departments?

4-8 To what extent is the success of your team affected by the activities of other teams or departments?

5—Decision Making

5-1 To what extent does the decision-making process in your organization encourage teams to seek and acquire more efficient equipment?

5-2 To what extent does the decision-making process in your organization encourage teams to seek and acquire more efficient technology?

5-3 To what extent is information widely shared so that those who make decisions have access to such information?

5-4 When decisions are being made, to what extent are the persons affected asked for their ideas? [14]

5-5 To what extent are decisions made at the levels where the most adequate and accurate information is available?

5-6 To what extent does management consult with team members before making a decision that may affect team activities? [14]

5-7 To what extent does your supervisor share a problem with relevant subordinates individually to get their opinion, and then make a decision?

5-8 To what extent does your supervisor share a problem with subordinates in a group meeting to obtain their opinion, and then make a decision?

5-9 To what extent does your supervisor share a problem with subordinates in a group meeting and attempt to reach a group consensus on a decision?

5-10 To what extent can you influence the decisions that affect your job?

5-11 To what extent does management try to get the opinions and ideas of people who work here? [14]

5-12 To what extent is there sufficient decision-making authority located in the divisions (field operations, profit centers, etc.)?

5-13 To what extent does management communicate the reasons for important decisions to your team? [3]

5-14 To what extent does your supervisor consult subordinates before making a decision that may affect their work? [3, 23]

5-15 To what extent is your team able to arrive at a consensus when working on controversial issues?

6—Demographics

Demographic questions should be used with great care and as sparingly as possible. We have found that the higher the number of demographic questions asked, the less likely survey participants are to answer questions honestly (because of the fear of being identified). This becomes a greater problem when you are surveying small populations or creating many breakdowns of the data that separate the population of respondents into very small groups.

Carefully evaluate the need to use demographic questions to support your survey objectives.

Possible team effectiveness demographic questions include:

6-1 To what type of _____ team do you presently belong?

Manufacturing example	Healthcare example	Banking example
1. Shop floor	1. Patient care	1. Customer relations
2. Clerical/office/administrative	2. Technical	2. Loan administration
3. Technical	3. Administrative	3. Information technology
4. Professional	4. Maintenance and supply	4. Product marketing
5. Management	5. Management	5. Systems and procedures

6-2 What is the area/function in which you work?

Manufacturing example	Healthcare example	Banking example
1. Production	1. Administration	1. Administration
2. Finance	2. Medical services	2. Branch operations
3. Administration	3. Nursing services	3. Commercial loans
4. Marketing	4. Professional/Technical	4. Fund management
5. Field sales	5. Staff support	5. Customer services
6. Distribution	6. Support services	6. Audit and proof
7. Human resources		7. Information technology
8. Information technology		8. Support services

6-3 What is your level in the organization?
  1. Non-supervisory hourly
  2. Non-supervisory salaried
  3. First line supervisor
  4. Manager
  5. Director
  6. Executive management

6-4   How long have you participated in a _____ team?
1. Not at all
2. Less than 6 months
3. 7 to 12 months
4. 13 to 18 months
5. 19 to 24 months
6. 2 to 3 years
7. More than 3 years

6-5   How long have you been employed by the organization?
1. Less than 6 months
2. 7 to 12 months
3. 1 to 2 years
4. 3 to 5 years
5. 6 to 10 years
6. 11 to 20 years
7. More than 20 years

6-6   What is your level of education?
1. Grade 8 or less
2. Grade 9 to 11
3. Completed high school
4. Some college education
5. Received a college associate's degree
6. Received a bachelor's degree
7. Received a master's degree

6-7   What is your age group?
1. Less than 20 years of age
2. 20 to 25 years of age
3. 26 to 30 years of age
4. 31 to 35 years of age
5. 36 to 45 years of age
6. 46 to 55 years of age
7. 56 years of age or older

6-8   What type of training have you received?
1. Team member
2. Team leader
3. Team facilitator
4. Steering committee member
5. Plant/operating unit coordinator
6. Orientation

6-9 What is your department?
1. Field sales
2. Marketing
3. Product sales
4. Distribution
5. Administration
6. Other

6-10 Your position is classified as:
1. Exempt.
2. Non-exempt.

6-11 How many employees do you supervise?
1. None
2. 1 to 5
3. 5 to 10
4. 10 to 20
5. 20 or more

6-12 On what shift do you usually work?
1. Swing shift
2. Split shift
3. Flex-time
4. First shift
5. Second shift
6. Third shift

6-13 Your department primarily deals with:
1. Units inside your division.
2. Units in other divisions (offices).
3. Units at the corporate office.
4. Field units.
5. Customers.

6-14 In the last [period of time], what is the number of problems your team has pursued (resolved)? [16, 20]
1. None
2. 1 to 2
3. 3 to 4
4. 5 to 10
5. More than 10

7—Facilitation

7-1 To what extent is your facilitator well trained to assist your team?

7-2 To what extent has the facilitator clearly explained his or her role?

7-3 To what extent is the facilitator effective in getting the group to focus on a common task?

7-4 To what extent is the facilitator effective in getting the group to use one method or procedure at a time?

7-5 To what extent does the facilitator help keep the meeting moving smoothly?

7-6 To what extent does the facilitator *avoid* talking too much?

7-7 To what extent does the facilitator protect group members and their ideas?

7-8 To what extent does the facilitator keep the team leader from dominating the meeting?

7-9 To what extent is the facilitator effective in dealing with disruptive behavior of participants?

7-10 To what extent is the facilitator able to remain neutral (not take sides)?

7-11 To what extent does the facilitator *avoid* becoming defensive when criticized?

7-12 To what extent does your team use your facilitator effectively?

8—Innovation and Creativity

8-1 To what extent have new opportunities been opened for the organization because people are encouraged to take calculated risks?

8-2 To what extent are people encouraged to take more personal responsibility in this organization?

8-3 To what extent are you encouraged to show initiative?

8-4 To what extent are you encouraged to exercise judgment?

8-5 To what extent are teams encouraged to initiate projects that are important in the organization?

8-6 To what extent does your job require that you keep learning new things?

8-7 To what extent are you asked for your ideas?

8-8 In your team, to what extent are cost-reducing ideas given consideration?

8-9 In your team, to what extent are cost-reducing ideas acted upon?

8-10 To what extent does management reward team members for innovation and calculated risk-taking?

8-11 To what extent is upper management supportive of your team pursuing ideas on its own?

8-12 To what extent do members ask open-ended or "what-if" questions to help the group look at the problem from a different perspective?

8-13 To what extent are you encouraged to be creative as you pursue solutions to problems?

8-14 To what extent do members of your team *avoid* criticizing others for proposing "different" or "far-out" ideas? [17]

8-15 To what extent do team members encourage innovative and creative ideas? [26]

8-16 To what extent are team members willing to take risks? [24]

8-17 To what extent do team members avoid belittling the contributions of others? [26]

9—Management

9-1 To what extent does top management in this organization support _____ teams? [13]

9-2 To what extent does management stress quality over quantity in this organization? [13]

9-3 To what extent do you know the quality standards or requirements of your job? [1, 13, 18]

9-4 To what extent does upper management actively and visibly support the _____ team process?

9-5 To what extent are your efforts as a _____ team participant appreciated within this organization? [11, 20, 22]

9-6 To what extent have improvements developed by your _____ team been given adequate consideration by management? [21]

9-7 To what extent have improvements suggested by your _____ team been implemented? [20]

9-8 To what extent have improvements identified by teams not resulted in the loss of employee jobs? [20]

9-9 To what extent does management view _____ teams as a way to develop employee skills?

9-10 To what extent does your team get a prompt response from management when you have a question?

9-11 To what extent has management been clear as to the goals of the _____ team process?

9-12 To what extent are there effective working relationships between management and _____ teams in this organization?

9-13 To what extent does your involvement in _____ teams lead to recognition and respect? [22]

9-14 To what extent was management receptive to your team's presentation(s)? [21]

9-15 To what extent is the team recognition program a meaningful way to recognize employee efforts? [22]

9-16 To what extent has management made _____ teams part of "the way we do business" in this organization? [24]

9-17 To what extent have members of management been adequately prepared to manage the _____ team process? [27]

9-18 To what extent are the requests for management presentations given prompt attention? [21]

9-19 To what extent is middle management not threatened by employee participation in _____ teams?

9-20 To what extent has there been a sufficient financial commitment to support the _____ team process?

9-21 To what extent does management respect the skills and abilities of employees?

9-22 To what extent is management looking over your shoulder to justify the results of the team process? [20, 21]

9-23 To what extent does management view _____ teams as a long-term process? [20]

9-24 To what extent does management act according to its statements about the importance of employees to the success of the company?

9-25 To what extent does management respect employees?

9-26 To what extent do employees respect management?

9-27 To what extent does management trust employees?

9-28 To what extent do employees trust management?

10—Meeting Practices

10-1   To what extent is the time spent in team meetings put to constructive use?

10-2   To what extent does the team *avoid* skipping from subject to subject?

10-3   To what extent do members of the team *avoid* raising concerns and questions that are off the subject?

10-4   To what extent do members use the meeting agenda to keep the meeting on track?

10-5   To what extent is the proper amount of information discussed so team members do not become overwhelmed?

10-6   To what extent do team members avoid coming and going at will during the meeting?

10-7   To what extent are the rules for conducting the meeting clear?

10-8   To what extent does discussion come to the point and not seem to go on endlessly?

10-9   To what extent are agendas prepared and sent out to all participants in advance of the meeting?

10-10 To what extent is there an appropriate number of agenda items for the time available?

10-11 To what extent are the objectives of the meeting clearly stated in the agenda so that participants come to the meeting with similar expectations?

10-12 To what extent do solutions to problems reflect the view of the entire team, not solely that of the leader?

10-13 To what extent is participation by all team members encouraged? [14, 17]

10-14 To what extent do all members of the team participate in discussions? [14, 17]

10-15 To what extent do all members get to air their concerns in team meetings? [17, 24]

10-16 To what extent do all sides of an issue get discussed? [3, 17]

10-17 To what extent do members *avoid* monopolizing the discussion? [17]

10-18 To what extent are the meetings you attend useful and necessary?

10-19 To what extent do the meetings you attend have a planned agenda?

10-20 To what extent does your team hold meetings to allow people to share information?

10-21 To what extent do all members get to see their ideas on the agenda for team meetings? [24]

10-22 To what extent does your team hold meetings to allow members to discuss current problems?

10-23 To what extent do team meetings provide an opportunity to review and discuss goals and objectives?

10-24 To what extent do team meetings focus on opportunities for improving individual and group performance?

10-25 To what extent does your team use group meetings to recognize high quality performance?

10-26 To what extent do team meetings include time for an evaluation of the effectiveness of the meeting? [17]

10-27 To what extent does your team use meeting time to solve problems of vital concern to the team?

10-28 To what extent do your team meetings begin on time?

10-29 To what extent do your team meetings end on time?

10-30 To what extent are your team meetings *not* canceled due to conflicting priorities?

10-31 To what extent does your team have access to suitable space to conduct team meetings?

10-32 To what extent do a few team members dominate team meetings? [17]

11—Member Role

11-1 To what extent would you like to participate in a _____ team? [13, 14]

11-2 To what extent are you concerned about product (service) quality? [18]

11-3 To what extent are your skills and abilities being used? [12]

11-4 To what extent do you understand your role in the _____ team process? [17, 27]

11-5 To what extent do you enjoy being a member of a _____ team? [14]

11-6 To what extent would you join another team if transferred to another department? [14]

11-7 To what extent would you recommend to others that they join a team? [14]

11-8 To what extent are your efforts as a _____ team participant appreciated within this organization? [9, 20, 22]

11-9 To what extent has your participation in a _____ team improved your skills?

11-10 To what extent do you have a chance to influence the goals that are set for your team?

11-11 To what extent are employees seen as experts in their work areas? [13]

11-12 To what extent has your participation in a _____ team increased your opportunity for further advancement? [20, 22]

11-13 To what extent will you be supportive of other employees who choose to participate in a _____ team?

11-14 To what extent are you interested in participating in the training that is part of the _____ team process? [14, 27]

12—Organization Conditions

12-1   To what extent is the work climate of this organization likely to support _____ teams? [13]

12-2   To what extent do different departments work together effectively to solve cross-functional problems? [13, 16]

12-3   To what extent does this organization have a real interest in the welfare and satisfaction of those who work here?

12-4   To what extent do you look forward to coming to work each day?

12-5   To what extent are there things about working here (people, policies, or conditions) that encourage you to work hard?

12-6   To what extent are you satisfied with your job?

12-7   To what extent are you satisfied with this organization?

12-8   To what extent are you satisfied with the pay for your job, compared with other jobs in the community that require the same skills?

12-9   To what extent are your skills and abilities being used? [11]

12-10 To what extent do you understand how your job fits in with other work going on in this organization? [2]

12-11 To what extent are the equipment and resources you have to work with adequate, efficient, and well maintained?

12-12 To what extent is the downward flow of information adequate in this organization? [3]

12-13 To what extent are trust and loyalty evident among people in this organization?

12-14 To what extent do you influence the goals that are set for your job? [14]

12-15 To what extent have clear, specific performance goals been established for your job? [1]

12-16 To what extent are your group meetings productive?

12-17 To what extent are you aware of the use of _____ teams or other employee involvement processes by our competitors?

13—Organization Readiness

13-1   To what extent are non-supervisory employees involved in solving work-related problems? [14]

13-2   To what extent *should* non-supervisory employees be involved in solving work-related problems? [14]

13-3   To what extent are employees in this organization willing to help solve work-related problems?

13-4   To what extent would you like to participate in a _____ team? [11, 14]

13-5   To what extent is your supervisor willing to allow you to participate in a _____ team? [14, 23]

13-6   To what extent can _____ teams improve product quality in this organization?

13-7   To what extent is the work climate of this organization likely to support _____ teams? [12]

13-8   To what extent will top management in this organization support _____ teams? [9]

13-9   To what extent do different departments work together effectively to solve cross-functional problems? [12, 16]

13-10   To what extent will cross-functional cooperation improve if the company adopts _____ teams? [20]

13-11   To what extent does this organization provide sufficient training for its employees? [27]

13-12   To what extent does management stress quality over quantity in this organization? [9]

13-13   To what extent do you know the quality standards or requirements of your job? [1, 9, 18]

13-14   To what extent is there emphasis on teamwork in this organization?

13-15   To what extent would the use of _____ teams increase your effectiveness? [18]

13-16   To what extent do you think of yourself as a member of a total organization team?

13-17   To what extent are employees seen as experts in their work areas? [11]

13-18   To what extent do employees have input on issues affecting the quality of their work life?

13-19   To what extent does the union adequately support _____ teams?

13-20   To what extent have you participated in this organization's suggestion program?

13-21   To what extent do you think the _____ team process will be a success in this organization?

13-22   To what extent are the organization's policies and procedures supportive of employee involvement? [2, 14]

13-23   To what extent are you aware of similar processes being implemented by competitors?

13-24   To what extent do employees want a greater degree of involvement in company improvement activities? [14]

13-25   To what extent has the proposed _____ team process been adequately communicated? [3]

14—Participation

14-1   To what extent do you influence the goals that are set for your job? [12]

14-2   To what extent are non-supervisory employees involved in solving work-related problems? [13]

14-3   To what extent *should* non-supervisory employees be involved in solving work related problems? [13]

14-4   To what extent would you like to participate in a _____ team? [11, 13]

14-5   To what extent is your supervisor willing to allow you to participate in a _____ team? [23]

14-6   To what extent are you asked for your thoughts/ideas on how to improve quality? [18]

14-7   To what extent do you feel free to suggest changes that would allow you to perform your job more effectively?

14-8   To what extent do changes occur as a result of your suggestions?

14-9   To what extent is your supervisor receptive to suggestions and ideas from your work group? [23]

14-10 When decisions are made, to what extent are persons affected asked for their ideas? [5]

14-11 To what extent does management consult with team members before making a decision that may affect team activities? [5]

14-12 To what extent are the organization's policies and procedures supportive of employee involvement? [2, 13]

14-13 To what extent is participation by all team members encouraged? [10, 17]

14-14 To what extent do all members of the team participate in discussions? [10, 17]

14-15 To what extent do you understand your role in the _____ team process? [11, 27]

14-16 To what extent do you enjoy being a member of a _____ team? [11]

14-17 To what extent would you want to join another team if transferred to another department? [11]

14-18 To what extent would you recommend to others that they join a team? [11]

14-19 To what extent are nonparticipating employees encouraged to join a team?

14-20 To what extent are you interested in participating in the training that is part of the _____ team process? [11, 27]

14-21 To what extent would you like to take a leadership role on a team?

14-22 To what extent do employees want a greater degree of involvement in company improvement activities? [13]

14-23 To what extent does management try to get the opinions and ideas of people who work here? [5]

15—Planning

15-1   To what extent are there specific goals for quality improvement in this organization?

15-2   To what extent do different units/departments/teams plan together and coordinate their efforts? [4]

15-3   To what extent does your supervisor help schedule work so you can participate in team activities? [23]

15-4   To what extent does your supervisor provide the help you need so that you can schedule work ahead of time? [23]

15-5 To what extent does your work group have specific, measurable goals for quality improvement?

15-6 To what extent does your _____ team plan together and coordinate its efforts?

15-7 To what extent does this organization plan its activities/efforts rather than react to events?

15-8 To what extent does the _____ team effort in this organization appear to be well planned?

15-9 To what extent does management emphasize the importance of planning in this organization?

15-10 To what extent does your supervisor spend sufficient time on planning?

15-11 To what extent does your _____ team spend sufficient time on planning?

15-12 To what extent does your _____ team measure results against established plans?

15-13 To what extent are the plans established in this organization realistic?

15-14 To what extent is your team free to develop its own problem-solving objectives? [24]

15-15 To what extent does your team focus on issues it can do something about? [16]

16—Problem Solving

16-1 To what extent do different departments work together effectively to solve cross-functional problems? [12, 13]

16-2 To what extent do teams and different departments work together effectively to solve cross-functional problems?

16-3 To what extent has your team been able to identify significant problems?

16-4 To what extent should employees participate in solving company problems?

16-5 To what extent does your team propose solutions after thoroughly identifying causes of problems?

16-6 To what extent are problems resolved rather than being revisited over the span of several meetings?

16-7 To what extent are various alternatives discussed before a decision is reached?

16-8 To what extent is there full agreement as to the real issue or problem being considered?

16-9 To what extent does the team select problems it could and/or should try to solve?

16-10 To what extent does the team select problems it has enough expertise or available information to analyze and solve?

16-11 To what extent does the team examine enough alternatives?

16-12 To what extent does the team *avoid* rushing prematurely to a decision?

16-13 To what extent does the team try to reach consensus on a solution?

16-14 When a decision is reached, to what extent is appropriate action taken? [20]

16-15 To what extent do changes in this organization *not* create more problems than they solve?

16-16 To what extent are your team members helpful in solving job-related problems?

16-17 To what extent do you have opportunities to work with others in solving job-related problems?

16-18 To what extent are work-related disagreements between team members accepted as normal?

16-19 To what extent are work-related disagreements between team members worked through rather than avoided?

16-20 To what extent does the team rely more heavily on group discussion rather than individual judgment?

16-21 To what extent are the *causes* of problems clearly identified and defined?

16-22 To what extent is identifying and solving problems considered an expected part of the job?

16-23 To what extent does management give recognition to team members when they solve a problem?

16-24 To what extent does management not keep you in the dark about things you need to know? [3]

16-25 To what extent are solutions to problems reached by consensus?

16-26 To what extent are problems *not* resolved by a "majority rule" or "rank has privilege"?

16-27 To what extent are real problems, rather than symptoms, the focus of problem-solving efforts?

16-28 To what extent does management *not* ignore problems in the hope that they will just disappear?

16-29 To what extent are problems dealt with at the proper level in the organization?

16-30 To what extent are team members well trained in group problem-solving skills? [27]

16-31 To what extent are group problem-solving skills used routinely in the organization? [17]

16-32 To what extent are interpersonal conflicts resolved skillfully?

16-33 To what extent is the use of effective feedback a part of problem solving in this organization? [17]

16-34 To what extent have _____ teams helped prevent problems before they arise? [20, 24]

16-35 In the last [period of time], what is the number of problems your team has pursued (resolved)? [6, 20]
  1. None
  2. 1 to 2
  3. 3 to 4
  4. 5 to 10
  5. More than 10

16-36 To what extent does your team identify *all* potential problems rather than settling on the most obvious one(s) for further consideration?

16-37 To what extent does your team focus on issues you can do something about? [15]

16-38 To what extent does your team make sure you are discussing the real problem?

16-39 To what extent does your team *avoid* jumping from stating the problem to proposing solutions?

16-40 To what extent does your team develop clear criteria that a solution must meet to be acceptable?

16-41 To what extent does your team search creatively for all reasonably promising solutions?

16-42 To what extent does your team seek innovative solutions by using different frames of reference to examine the problem?

16-43 To what extent does your team separate the discovery and listing of solutions from their evaluation?

16-44 To what extent does your team use backup and recycling techniques when the group cannot reach consensus?

16-45 To what extent does your team recheck the proposed solution for undesirable side effects?

16-46 To what extent does your team take each problem-solving step in sequence?

17—Process Skills

17-1 To what extent is participation by all team members encouraged? [10, 14]

17-2 To what extent do all members of the team participate in discussions? [10, 14]

17-3 To what extent do all members get to air their concerns in team meetings? [10, 24]

17-4 To what extent do all members see their ideas on the agenda for team meetings? [3, 13]

17-5 To what extent do all sides of an issue get discussed? [3, 10]

17-6 To what extent do members *avoid* monopolizing the discussion? [10]

17-7 To what extent do members share full information with the leader rather than what he or she wants to hear? [24, 25]

17-8 To what extent are members willing to express their *real* views about problems or issues?

17-9 To what extent is disagreement or discord recognized and resolved?

17-10 To what extent are members treated with friendliness and respect?

17-11 To what extent are the minutes of team meetings prepared promptly? [19, 24]

17-12 To what extent is it clear as to who is responsible for action steps following the meeting? [24]

17-13 To what extent is your team knowledgeable about group dynamics?

17-14 To what extent do team meetings include time for an evaluation of the effectiveness of the meeting? [10]

17-15 To what extent are group problem-solving skills used routinely in your team? [16]

17-16 To what extent is the use of effective feedback a part of problem solving in this organization? [16]

17-17 To what extent does your team follow the rules of brainstorming?

17-18 To what extent do members of your team listen effectively when others in the team are speaking?

17-19 To what extent do members of your team use restatement to clarify discussions and ensure common understanding?

17-20 To what extent do members of your team accept another member's point of view even though they may not agree?

17-21 To what extent are minutes of team meetings prepared, in sufficient detail, to accurately document what happened during the meeting? [19]

17-22 To what extent has your team established effective guidelines for conducting team meetings?

17-23 To what extent do members of your team *avoid* criticizing others for proposing "different" or "far-out" ideas? [8]

17-24 To what extent do team members ask questions that help clarify the subject being discussed?

17-25 To what extent is feedback focused on behavior rather than the individual?

17-26 To what extent do team members *avoid* arguing only for their own solution?

17-27 To what extent do a few team members dominate team meetings? [10]

17-28 To what extent do team members attempt to summarize discussions and keep them on track?

17-29 To what extent does your team specify how, by whom, and when action is to be taken to implement the solution?

17-30 To what extent do team members listen to each other? [26]

17-31 To what extent do team members with differing viewpoints express themselves freely and fully? [24]

17-32 To what extent has your team built group cohesiveness prior to tackling hard problems, by tackling easy problems first? [24]

17-33 To what extent do team members *avoid* insisting that their views be accepted? [26]

17-34 To what extent do team members encourage the group to work through disagreements rather than suppress them? [26]

17-35 To what extent do team members *avoid* imposing decisions on the group? [24]

18—Quality

18-1 To what extent does this organization attempt to correct the cause of quality problems? [1]

18-2 To what extent is this organization concerned with product (service) quality?

18-3 To what extent are you concerned about product (service) quality? [11]

18-4 To what extent has the quality of your work improved because of the organization's _____ team process?

18-5 To what extent has the quality of the organization's products/services improved because of the _____ team process?

18-6 To what extent is providing good service to customers a top priority of organization employees?

18-7 To what extent do organization policies help you provide good service to customers?

18-8 To what extent do you feel free to suggest changes that would result in providing better service to customers?

18-9 To what extent do people in this organization care about providing good service to customers?

18-10 To what extent is providing a quality product to customers a top priority of organization employees?

18-11 To what extent do company policies help you produce a quality product?

18-12 To what extent do you feel free to suggest changes that would result in providing a better product/service to customers?

18-13 To what extent do people in this organization care about producing a quality product?

18-14 To what extent would the use of _____ teams increase your effectiveness? [13]

18-15 To what extent does the organization try to follow up on service by talking to customers? [3]

18-16 In your department, to what extent are new ideas that can improve service acted upon favorably? [20, 23]

18-17 To what extent do you try to improve the quality of the organization's products?

18-18 To what extent do you know the quality standards or requirements of your job? [1, 9, 13]

18-19 To what extent is scrap or rework a problem in this organization?

18-20 Since becoming a member of a _____ team, to what extent are you more conscious of the quality of your work?

18-21 To what extent are you asked for your thoughts/ideas on how to improve quality? [14]

18-22 To what extent does this organization respond to employee concerns about quality? [1]

18-23 To what extent does this organization respond to customer concerns about quality? [1]

18-24 To what extent are people in this organization held accountable for producing quality work? [1]

18-25 To what extent are you held accountable for producing quality work? [1]

18-26 To what extent does this organization try to improve quality? [1]

19—Recording

19-1 To what extent has the recorder defined his or her role/function at the beginning of the meeting?

19-2 To what extent does the recorder make sure meeting minutes are legible?

19-3 To what extent does the recorder capture the basic ideas of the meeting?

19-4 To what extent does the recorder make corrections without getting defensive?

19-5 To what extent does the recorder assist the group in organizing the data generated during the meeting?

19-6 To what extent are the minutes of team meetings prepared and distributed promptly? [17, 24]

19-7 To what extent are the minutes of team meetings prepared, in sufficient detail, to accurately document what happened during the meeting? [17]

20—Results

20-1 To what extent will cross-functional cooperation improve if the organization adopts _____ teams? [13]

20-2 To what extent has your team made a worthwhile contribution to the organization? [24]

20-3 To what extent are your efforts as a _____ team participant appreciated within this organization? [9, 11, 22]

20-4 To what extent is your relationship with others in your work group better than it has been in the past as a result of team activities?

20-5 To what extent are you better able to communicate with management now than in the past? [3]

20-6 To what extent have improvements suggested by your _____ team been implemented? [9]

20-7 To what extent are team successes recognized in the organization? [3, 22]

20-8 To what extent have improvements identified by teams not resulted in the loss of employee jobs? [9]

20-9 To what extent has your participation in teams improved your skills?

20-10 To what extent have your team's recommendations been accepted?

20-11 To what extent has the organization experienced cost savings because of the team program?

20-12 When a decision is reached, to what extent is appropriate action taken? [16]

20-13 In your department, to what extent are new ideas that can improve service acted upon favorably? [18, 23]

20-14 To what extent are you as productive as you could be? [2]

20-15 If you perform better on your job, to what extent will you have more job security?

20-16 To what extent do those persons/teams who successfully reduce costs receive recognition, promotion, or other rewards? [22]

20-17 To what extent has employee morale improved as a result of the _____ team process?

20-18 To what extent have _____ teams helped prevent problems? [16, 24]

20-19 To what extent has your participation in a _____ team increased your opportunity for further advancement? [11, 22]

20-20 As a result of the _____ team process, to what extent does management have an increased interest in and understanding of employees and their concerns?

20-21 In the last [period of time], what is the number of problems your team has pursued (resolved)? [6, 16]

   1. None
   2. One
   3. Two
   4. Three to four
   5. Five or more

20-22 To what extent are you satisfied that the time you have devoted to team activities has been worthwhile? [24]

20-23 To what extent have successful teams been identified as role models for the rest of the organization? [3, 22]

20-24 To what extent have managers who support _____ teams been identified as role models for the rest of the organization? [3, 23]

20-25 To what extent has the experience gained by individual teams been shared with all other teams to improve the entire process? [3]

20-26 To what extent have the results achieved by teams been adequately communicated? [3]

20-27 To what extent has an emphasis on quality improvement become part of the way work is done in the organization?

20-28 To what extent do team members *avoid* being impatient with the progress being made by the team? [24]

20-29 To what extent is management looking over your shoulder to justify the results of the team process? [9, 21]

20-30 To what extent does management view _____ teams as a long-term process? [9]

20-31 To what extent is your team being excessively pressured to produce short-term results?

20-32 To what extent is there an overemphasis on increased productivity in the team process?

20-33 To what extent have teams helped improve relations between management and the union?

20-34 To what extent do you understand how the _____ team process benefits the company? [24]

20-35 To what extent do you understand how the quality process benefits employees? [24]

21—Review

21-1   To what extent is your work measured against specific performance standards?

21-2   To what extent is your work measured against specific quality standards?

21-3   To what extent was management receptive to your team's presentation(s)? [9]

21-4   To what extent does management provide adequate time to review your team's efforts?

21-5   To what extent is your involvement in a _____ team considered in your performance appraisal?

21-6   To what extent is doing quality work important in your performance appraisal?

21-7   To what extent does your supervisor provide guidance so that you can improve your performance? [23]

21-8   To what extent are the requests for management presentations given prompt attention? [9]

21-9   To what extent is management looking over your shoulder to justify the results of the team process? [9, 20]

21-10 To what extent do team meetings include time for an evaluation of the effectiveness of the meeting?

21-11 To what extent does your team leader help define the results expected of your team? [23, 25]

21-12 To what extent is the union adequately involved in reviewing _____ team activities?

21-13 To what extent is your supervisor effective in following through on activities/assignments to ensure accurate/timely completion? [23]

21-14 To what extent have improvements developed by your _____ team been given adequate consideration by management? [9]

22—Rewards

22-1   To what extent is doing the job right the first time more important than just getting it done?

22-2   To what extent does this organization reward people for doing a quality job?

22-3   To what extent is producing a quality product/service for our customers important in this organization?

22-4   To what extent is your supervisor free with praise for work that is of high quality? [3, 23]

22-5   To what extent have successful teams been identified as role models for the rest of the organization? [3, 20]

22-6   To what extent do team members give credit and recognition generously? [26]

22-7   To what extent are your efforts as a _____ team participant appreciated within this organization? [9, 11, 20]

22-8   To what extent does your involvement in _____ teams lead to recognition and respect? [9]

22-9   To what extent is the team recognition program a meaningful way to reward employee efforts? [9]

22-10 To what extent has your participation in a _____ team increased your opportunity for further advancement? [11, 20]

22-11 To what extent are team successes recognized in this organization? [3, 20]

22-12 To what extent do those persons/teams who successfully reduce costs receive recognition, promotion, or other rewards? [20]

22-13 To what extent does your supervisor give you sufficient recognition when you do a good job? [23]

23—Supervision

23-1   To what extent is your supervisor willing to allow you to participate in a _____ team? [14]

23-2   To what extent does your supervisor support your involvement in the team?

23-3   To what extent does your supervisor help schedule work so you can participate in team activities? [15]

23-4   In your department, to what extent are new ideas that can improve service acted upon favorably? [18, 20]

23-5   To what extent does your supervisor encourage people to give their best effort?

23-6   To what extent does your supervisor maintain high standards of performance? [1]

23-7   To what extent does your supervisor hold you accountable for achieving high, but realistic, performance goals? [1]

23-8   To what extent is your supervisor free with praise for work that is of high quality? [3, 22]

23-9   To what extent does your supervisor expect you to find and correct your own errors?

23-10 To what extent does your supervisor encourage people to work together to solve problems?

23-11 To what extent does your team leader help define the results expected of your team? [21, 25]

23-12 To what extent does your supervisor provide guidance so that you can improve your performance? [21]

23-13 To what extent does your supervisor provide training so that you can improve your performance?

23-14 To what extent does your supervisor provide the help you need so that you can schedule work ahead of time? [15]

23-15 To what extent does your supervisor offer new ideas for solving job-related problems?

23-16 To what extent are you given the information you need to know to do your job in the best possible way? [3]

23-17 To what extent does your supervisor give you sufficient recognition when you do a good job? [22]

23-18 To what extent is your supervisor effective in following through on activities/assignments to ensure accurate/timely completion? [21]

23-19 To what extent is your supervisor friendly and easy to approach?

23-20 When you talk with your supervisor, to what extent does he or she pay attention to what you are saying?

23-21 To what extent is your supervisor willing to listen to your problems?

23-22 To what extent is your supervisor receptive to suggestions and ideas from your work group? [14]

23-23 To what extent does your supervisor have confidence and trust in you?

23-24 To what extent do you have confidence and trust in your supervisor?

23-25 To what extent does your supervisor encourage you to make suggestions?

23-26 If you went to your supervisor to inform him or her of an important mistake that you and/or your coworker(s) made, to what extent would your supervisor give support in resolving the problem?

23-27 To what extent does your supervisor express interest and concern for the people who work for him or her?

23-28 To what extent have managers who support _____ teams been identified as role models for the rest of the company? [3, 20]

23-29 To what extent does your supervisor encourage work group members to work as a team?

23-30 To what extent does your supervisor encourage work group members to exchange opinions and ideas on job-related problems?

23-31 To what extent does your supervisor treat everyone fairly?

23-32 To what extent does your supervisor consult subordinates before making a decision that may affect their work? [3, 5]

24—Team Functioning

24-1 To what extent is your team doing important work?

24-2 To what extent has your team made a worthwhile contribution to the organization? [20]

To what extent have each of the following contributed to the work of your team?

24-3 Yourself

24-4 Other team members

24-5 Team leader

24-6 Facilitator

24-7 Steering committee

24-8 Unit supervisor

24-9 Plant management

24-10 Corporate management

24-11 Union leadership

24-12 To what extent is adequate support provided when your team needs help?

24-13 To what extent do you understand what problems your team can work on?

24-14 To what extent do you understand what problems your team should not work on?

24-15 To what extent do all members get to air their concerns in team meetings? [10, 17]

24-16 To what extent do all members get to see their ideas on the agenda for team meetings? [10]

24-17 To what extent do members share full information with the leader rather than what he or she wants to hear? [17, 25]

24-18 To what extent are the meeting minutes prepared promptly? [17, 19]

24-19 To what extent is it clear as to who is responsible for action steps following the meeting? [17]

24-20 How often does [should] your team meet?

    1. Daily
    2. More than once a week, but not daily
    3. Once a week
    4. Twice a month
    5. Once a month
    6. Less than once a month

24-21 For what length of time does [should] your team meet?

    1. Less than an hour
    2. Approximately one hour
    3. Between one and two hours
    4. More than two hours

24-22 To what extent have _____ teams helped prevent problems before they arise? [16, 20]

24-23 To what extent is your team able to effectively identify problems in your work area?

24-24 To what extent is the work of your team equally shared among all team participants?

24-25 To what extent has your team shifted its emphasis from problem solving to problem prevention?

24-26 To what extent are members of your team serious about making the _____ team process work?

24-27 To what extent is your team effective in collecting required data for charting and problem solving?

24-28 To what extent is there adequate follow-up on assignments between team meetings?

24-29 To what extent has the [coordinating group] given your team adequate attention?

24-30 To what extent is the [coordinating group] effective in providing direction for the team process?

24-31 To what extent are you satisfied that the time you have devoted to team activities has been worthwhile? [20]

24-32 To what extent have the goals of the _____ team process been clearly defined?

24-33 To what extent do you understand how the _____ team process benefits the organization? [20]

24-34 To what extent do you understand how the _____ team process benefits employees? [20]

24-35 To what extent has management made _____ teams part of "the way we do business" in this organization? [9]

24-36 To what extent do team members with differing viewpoints express themselves freely and fully? [17]

24-37 To what extent has your team built group cohesiveness prior to tackling hard problems, by tackling easy problems first? [17]

24-38 To what extent do team members avoid imposing decisions on the group? [17]

24-39 To what extent do team members deemphasize status? [26]

24-40 To what extent do team members use the authority of facts, rather than the authority of persons, in developing a course of action? [26]

24-41 To what extent do team members think what the team is doing is important? [26]

24-42 To what extent are team members willing to take risks? [8]

24-43 To what extent do team members avoid being impatient with the progress being made by the team? [20]

24-44 To what extent is your team free to develop its own problem-solving objectives? [15]

24-45 To what extent is there not an overemphasis on cost savings in the _____ team process?

25—Team Leadership

25-1 To what extent has the leader clearly explained his or her role in the _____ team process?

25-2 To what extent is the leader effective in getting the group to focus on a common task?

25-3 To what extent is the leader effective in getting the group to use one method or procedure at a time?

25-4 To what extent does the leader help keep the meeting moving smoothly?

25-5 To what extent does the leader *avoid* talking too much?

25-6 To what extent is the leader effective in dealing with disruptive behavior of participants?

25-7 To what extent is the leader effective in bringing the group to closure and agreement on specific action items?

25-8 To what extent do members share full information with the leader rather than what he or she wants to hear? [17, 24]

25-9   To what extent are your team meetings productive?

25-10 To what extent does your team leader arrange work for the most effective handling of assignments?

25-11 To what extent does your team leader help define the results expected of your team? [21, 23]

25-12 To what extent does your team leader maintain high standards of performance? [1]

25-13 To what extent does your team leader listen well to team members whether he or she agrees or disagrees with what is being said?

Note: Several questions in the Supervision category (23) can be modified for use in assessing team leadership characteristics.

26—Team Member Interaction

26-1   To what extent do persons on your team encourage each other to give their best efforts?

26-2   To what extent do persons on your team maintain high standards of performance? [1]

26-3   To what extent are members of your team pleased when you improve your performance?

26-4   To what extent do team members expect you to do your very best?

26-5   To what extent do team members think what the team is doing is important? [24]

26-6   To what extent do persons on your team help you find ways to do a better job?

26-7   To what extent do persons on your team provide the information you need so that you can plan [organize] [schedule] work ahead of time?

26-8   To what extent do team members cooperate with each other?

26-9   To what extent do persons on your team offer each other new ideas for solving job-related problems?

26-10 How friendly and easy to approach are persons on your team?

26-11 When you talk with persons on your team, to what extent do they pay attention to what you are saying?

26-12 To what extent do team members listen to each other? [17]

26-13 To what extent do team members *avoid* insisting that their views be accepted? [17]

26-14 To what extent do team members treat each member's contribution as important?

26-15 To what extent do team members encourage innovative and creative ideas? [8]

26-16 To what extent do team members *avoid* belittling the contributions of others? [8]

26-17 To what extent do team members *avoid* treating others in a condescending manner?

26-18 To what extent do persons on your team encourage each other to work as a team?

26-19 To what extent do persons on your team work toward *team* goals?

26-20 To what extent is there freedom from favoritism in your team?

26-21 To what extent is there teamwork in your team?

26-22 To what extent do you consider yourself a member of a well-functioning team?

26-23 To what extent do team members help you in solving job-related problems?

26-24 To what extent do team members encourage the group to work through disagreements rather than suppress them? [17]

26-25 To what extent do team members deemphasize status? [24]

26-26 To what extent do team members use the authority of facts, rather than the authority of persons, in developing a course of action? [24]

26-27 To what extent do team members use "we" and "our" rather than "I" or "any" in their discussions?

26-28 To what extent do team members give credit and recognition generously? [22]

27—Training

27-1 To what extent does this organization provide sufficient training for its employees? [13]

27-2 To what extent was _____ well prepared to present _____?

27-3 To what extent were the course materials well written and easily understood?

27-4 To what extent was _____ knowledgeable of the subject?

27-5 To what extent did you receive clear answers to your questions?

27-6 To what extent was adequate time provided to cover the material?

27-7 To what extent do you have a good understanding of the team process in this company?

27-8 To what extent do you understand your role in the _____ team process? [11, 14]

27-9 To what extent are you well prepared to participate in a team?

27-10 To what extent were the _____ training sessions interesting and able to keep your attention?

27-11 To what extent were the training visual aids clear and well prepared?

27-12 To what extent was the training well organized?

27-13 To what extent was the training provided in a comfortable setting?

27-14 To what extent were you adequately trained prior to joining the team?

27-15 To what extent was your overall level of training adequate prior to joining the team?

27-16 To what extent does the training function provide adequate assistance to your team?

27-17 To what extent are team members well trained in group problem-solving skills? [16]

27-18 To what extent have ongoing training and support been sufficient to continue your skill development?

To what extent do you understand how to create a:

27-19 Fishbone diagram?

27-20 Pie chart?

27-21 Line graph?

27-22 Histogram?

27-23 Pareto graph?

27-24 Process flow chart?

27-25 To what extent do you understand the concept of cost effectiveness?

27-26 To what extent would you like to have additional training in more sophisticated problem-solving and project-management techniques?

27-27 To what extent have members of management been adequately prepared to manage the _____ team process? [9]

27-28 To what extent are _____ team leaders trained to deal effectively with the politics of the organization?

27-29 To what extent do you understand how to construct a valid sample for data collection purposes?

27-30 To what extent do you understand how to use a weighting factor for data analysis?

27-31 To what extent are team members well trained in group problem-solving skills?

27-32 To what extent do you understand how to construct a check sheet for data collection purposes?

27-33 To what extent do you know how to plot a cumulative frequency line?

27-34 To what extent do you know how to create a scatter gram?

27-35 To what extent do you understand the concept of standard deviation?

27-36 To what extent are you interested in participating in the training that is part of the _____ team process? [11, 14]

Prior to joining the team [since joining the team], to what extent had [have] you been adequately trained in each of the following skills?

27-37 Decision making

27-38 Fishbone analysis

27-39 Graphs

27-40 Statistics

27-41 Conducting a meeting

27-42 Team interaction

27-43 Interpersonal relations

27-44 Management philosophy

27-45 Goal-setting processes

27-46 Project planning

27-47 Report writing

27-48 Oral presentations

28—Written Comment Questions

28-1 What are the strengths of the team training program?

28-2 What do you think could be done to improve the training process?

28-3   What are the strengths of the _____ team process in this organization?

28-4   What causes the team process to be less effective than it could be?

28-5   What would you suggest be done to improve the effectiveness of the team process?

28-6   Other comments you may wish to make about the team process.

28-7   What could management do to improve the _____ team process?

28-8   Other comments you may wish to make regarding the implementation of _____ teams at _____.

Section 3

Sample Survey Questionnaires

To demonstrate how a questionnaire can be developed, we have selected representative questions from Section 2 and have created three sample surveys. These surveys can be used to assess three phases of a team program/process: organization readiness, process implementation, and meeting practices.

Each organization implements its team program/process somewhat differently. For example, the name of the process, the scope and focus of the effort, and the content of the training may vary greatly among organizations. The surveys included in the section *are designed as examples* to illustrate typical survey questionnaires. The focus of these surveys is on quality teams; however, similar instruments can be developed to suit a wide variety of information needs relating to cross-functional teams, corrective action teams, method-specific teams (Six Sigma, lean, quality function deployment, strategy deployment, and so forth), or any other problem-solving or employee involvement group.

THE TEAM READINESS SURVEY

This survey is designed for use prior to the introduction of the team program/process and provides an indication of employee and management readiness to participate in and support the process. This type of survey is generally administered organization-wide, either to the total employee population or a random sample. It can be repeated to determine if readiness has improved to a point where the organization is ready to commit the resources to a team program/process.

THE TEAM IMPLEMENTATION SURVEY

This survey is designed to be administered a few months after the team program/process has been implemented, in order to determine how well it is working in the organization. This type of survey usually is conducted periodically to monitor ongoing team activities and at key team milestones. This survey can be developed at the team level to measure items that are of specific interest to the team members, or it can be developed as an organization-wide survey when comparison of team efforts is deemed necessary. Please note that if it is left to individual teams to develop the survey, no comparison across teams will be possible.

THE TEAM MEETING EFFECTIVENESS SURVEY

This survey is designed to assess team program/process meeting practices and provide feedback as to how the team is functioning. This type of assessment may be conducted as often as deemed necessary. However, we suggest using this questionnaire at least twice a year to ensure that improvement efforts are kept current with the needs of the team.

The survey questionnaires can be constructed using recent versions of Microsoft Word. A blank questionnaire template is contained in Section 4 and can be used to create your own survey questionnaire. An electronic version of the survey template is also included on the CD-ROM that accompanies this workbook. This form will meet your needs if you use a 5-point *extent* scale for survey responses. Should you choose to use another type of scale, you can easily develop a suitable form to meet your specifications.

Cadbury Enterprises

SAMPLE SURVEY

Team Readiness Survey

You are about to take part in a very important task. The answers that you give to the questions in this survey will provide important information for management of Cadbury Enterprises as they consider the use of TEAMS in the company.

To protect confidentiality, no names are to be placed on the survey. To help in the analysis of the survey results, you will be asked to provide your work location and work level.

Thank you for your time and assistance in completing this important task.

Instructions

1. Each question has five possible responses. Please circle the number corresponding to your response choice for each question. If you do not find a response choice that fits your exact view, choose the one closest to it.

2. If you find a question where you have no information on which to base an answer, skip the question and go on to the next question. We encourage you to answer all questions, if possible.

3. Commonly used terms in this survey mean the following:
   –Supervisor—the person to whom you generally report
   –Organization—Cadbury Enterprises

4. There is no time limit for taking this survey. Please take the time to read each question carefully before you answer.

Before starting the survey, please provide us with the following information to help in the analysis of the survey results:

Your four-digit work location code number				

Please check your level in Cadbury Enterprises: (Check only one)

	Non-supervisory, hourly
	Non-supervisory, salaried
	First-line supervisor
	Middle management
	Vice-president/executive management

Cadbury Enterprises

Team Readiness Survey

		1. To a Very Little Extent	2. To a Little Extent	3. To Some Extent	4. To a Great Extent	5. To a Very Great Extent
1.	To what extent does this organization have a real interest in the welfare and satisfaction of those who work here?	1	2	3	4	5
2.	To what extent do you look forward to coming to work each day?	1	2	3	4	5
3.	To what extent do you understand how your job fits in with other work going on in this organization?	1	2	3	4	5
4.	To what extent are the equipment and resources you work with adequate, efficient, and well maintained?	1	2	3	4	5
5.	To what extent are your skills and abilities being used?	1	2	3	4	5
6.	To what extent would increased teamwork benefit this organization?	1	2	3	4	5
7.	To what extent does this organization provide sufficient training for its employees?	1	2	3	4	5
8.	To what extent is this organization concerned about product/service quality?	1	2	3	4	5
9.	To what extent is there an emphasis on teamwork in this organization?	1	2	3	4	5
10.	To what extent can employees influence issues affecting the quality of their work life?	1	2	3	4	5
11.	To what extent are non-supervisory employees in this organization involved in solving work-related problems?	1	2	3	4	5
12.	To what extent should non-supervisory employees be involved in solving work-related problems?	1	2	3	4	5
13.	To what extent is the work climate or culture of this organization likely to support team activities?	1	2	3	4	5
14.	To what extent do different departments work together effectively to solve cross-departmental problems?	1	2	3	4	5
15.	To what extent does management stress product/service quality over quantity in this organization?	1	2	3	4	5
16.	Communication is a two-way street: To what extent does management listen as well as talk?	1	2	3	4	5

Cadbury Enterprises

Team Readiness Survey

| 5. To a Very Great Extent |
| 4. To a Great Extent |
| 3. To Some Extent |
| 2. To a Little Extent |
| 1. To a Very Little Extent |

17.	To what extent would you like to see a team approach to improve product/service quality in this organization?	1	2	3	4	5
18.	To what extent is top management likely to support team activities in this organization?	1	2	3	4	5
19.	To what extent is your supervisor willing to allow you to participate in team activities?	1	2	3	4	5
20.	To what extent is your supervisor supportive of the team concept?	1	2	3	4	5
21.	To what extent would you like to take a leadership role in team activities?	1	2	3	4	5
22.	To what extent do you understand how team activities can benefit this organization?	1	2	3	4	5
23.	To what extent do you think team activities will be a success in this organization?	1	2	3	4	5
24.	To what extent has the proposed team activity concept for this organization been adequately communicated to you?	1	2	3	4	5

Written Comments

In the space below, please provide any comments you wish to make regarding the proposed implementation of a team process at Cadbury Enterprises.

Thank you for your participation in this survey.

Cadbury Enterprises

SAMPLE SURVEY

Team Implementation Survey

You are about to take part in a very important task. The answers that you give to the questions in this survey will provide important information for management of Cadbury Enterprises as they evaluate the use of *CETeams* in the company.

To protect confidentiality, no names are to be placed on the survey. To help in the analysis of the survey results, you will be asked to provide your work location and work level.

Thank you for your time and assistance in completing this important task.

Instructions

1. Each question has five possible responses. Please circle the number corresponding to your response choice for each question. If you do not find a response choice that fits your exact view, choose the one closest to it.

2. If you find a question where you have no information on which to base an answer, skip the question and go on to the next question. We encourage you to answer all questions, if possible.

3. Commonly used terms in this survey mean the following:

   –Supervisor—the person to whom you generally report

   –*CETeam*—a group composed of Cadbury Enterprises' members, sometimes from different departments or areas, assigned a specific activity or task

4. There is no time limit for taking this survey. Please take the time to read each question carefully before you answer.

Before starting the survey, please provide us with the following information to help in the analysis of the survey results:

Your four-digit *CETeam* code number				

Cadbury Enterprises

Team Implementation Survey

		5. To a Very Great Extent				
		4. To a Great Extent				
		3. To Some Extent				
		2. To a Little Extent				
		1. To a Very Little Extent				
1.	To what extent do you enjoy being a member of a *CETeam*?	1	2	3	4	5
2.	To what extent are *CETeam* successes recognized at Cadbury Enterprises?	1	2	3	4	5
3.	To what extent would you recommend to others that they join a *CETeam*?	1	2	3	4	5
4.	To what extent is your *CETeam* doing important work?	1	2	3	4	5
5.	To what extent is the time spent in *CETeam* meetings put to constructive use?	1	2	3	4	5
6.	To what extent does your supervisor support your involvement in *CETeam* activities?	1	2	3	4	5
7.	To what extent does your supervisor help schedule work so you can participate in *CETeam* activities?	1	2	3	4	5
8.	To what extent has your *CETeam* made a worthwhile contribution to Cadbury Enterprises?	1	2	3	4	5
9.	To what extent does upper management actively and visibly support the *CETeam* process?	1	2	3	4	5
10.	To what extent are your efforts as a *CETeam* participant appreciated at Cadbury Enterprises?	1	2	3	4	5
11.	To what extent is your relationship with others in your work group better than it has been in the past as a result of *CETeam* activities?	1	2	3	4	5
12.	To what extent have improvements developed by your *CETeam* been given adequate consideration by management?	1	2	3	4	5
13.	To what extent have improvements recommended by your *CETeam* been implemented?	1	2	3	4	5
14.	To what extent has your participation in *CETeam* activities increased your skills and abilities?	1	2	3	4	5
15.	To what extent does your *CETeam* facilitator appear to have training in the skills necessary to assist your team?	1	2	3	4	5

Cadbury Enterprises

Team Implementation Survey

	To what extent have you been properly trained in the following:	1. To a Very Little Extent	2. To a Little Extent	3. To Some Extent	4. To a Great Extent	5. To a Very Great Extent
16.	Decision-making and problem-solving skills?	1	2	3	4	5
17.	Six Sigma strategy and methodology?	1	2	3	4	5
18.	Group process skills?	1	2	3	4	5
19.	Group meeting skills?	1	2	3	4	5
20.	Project planning and implementation skills?	1	2	3	4	5
21.	Pareto analysis techniques?	1	2	3	4	5
22.	Basic statistics and graphing techniques?	1	2	3	4	5
23.	Report writing skills?	1	2	3	4	5
24.	Report presentation skills?	1	2	3	4	5

Written Comments

In the space below, please provide any comments you wish to make regarding how the *CETeam* process could be improved at Cadbury Enterprises.

Thank you for your participation in this survey.

Cadbury Enterprises

SAMPLE SURVEY

Team Meeting Effectiveness Survey

You are about to take part in a very important task. The answers that you give to the questions in this survey will provide important information for management of Cadbury Enterprises as they evaluate the use of *CETeams* in the company.

To protect confidentiality, no names are to be placed on the survey. To help in the analysis of the survey results, you will be asked to provide your work location and work level.

Thank you for your time and assistance in completing this important task.

Instructions

1. Each question has five possible responses. Please circle the number corresponding to your response choice for each question. If you do not find a response choice that fits your exact view, choose the one closest to it.

2. If you find a question where you have no information on which to base an answer, skip the question and go on to the next question. We encourage you to answer all questions, if possible.

3. Commonly used terms in this survey mean the following:

   –CETeam—a group composed of Cadbury Enterprises' members, sometimes from different departments or areas, assigned a specific activity or task

   –Steering Committee—Cadbury Enterprises' members who are responsible for overseeing your CETeam activities

4. There is no time limit for taking this survey. Please take the time to read each question carefully before you answer.

Before starting the survey, please provide us with the following information to help in the analysis of the survey results:

Your four-digit *CETeam* code number				

Cadbury Enterprises

**Team Meeting
Effectiveness Survey**

		1. To a Very Little Extent	2. To a Little Extent	3. To Some Extent	4. To a Great Extent	5. To a Very Great Extent
1.	To what extent is an agenda prepared and sent out in advance of your *CETeam* meetings?	1	2	3	4	5
2.	To what extent do *CETeam* members use a meeting agenda to keep the meeting on track?	1	2	3	4	5
3.	To what extent is there an appropriate number of agenda items compared to the time available?	1	2	3	4	5
4.	To what extent do your *CETeam* meetings start on time?	1	2	3	4	5
5.	To what extent do *all* your *CETeam* members attend meetings?	1	2	3	4	5
6.	To what extent do *all* your *CETeam* members effectively participate in your *CETeam* meetings?	1	2	3	4	5
7.	To what extent does your *CETeam* use effective planning, problem solving, and decision-making techniques?	1	2	3	4	5
8.	To what extent is the role of your *CETeam* leader clearly understood?	1	2	3	4	5
9.	To what extent is your *CETeam* leader performing his or her role effectively?	1	2	3	4	5
10.	To what extent does your *CETeam* use its meeting time effectively?	1	2	3	4	5
11.	To what extent is your *CETeam* producing the results expected of it?	1	2	3	4	5
12.	To what extent do you receive needed assistance from other groups or *CETeam*?	1	2	3	4	5
13.	To what extent do your steering committee members make themselves available when needed by your *CETeam*?	1	2	3	4	5
14.	To what extent does your steering committee make decisions promptly on your *CETeam* recommendations?	1	2	3	4	5
15.	To what extent are accurate minutes kept in your *CETeam* meetings?	1	2	3	4	5
16.	To what extent are meeting decisions and follow-up activities clearly identified in the *CETeam* meeting minutes?	1	2	3	4	5
17.	To what extent do your *CETeam* meetings end on time?	1	2	3	4	5
18.	To what extent are meeting minutes promptly distributed to *CETeam* members?	1	2	3	4	5

		1. To a Very Little Extent	2. To a Little Extent	3. To Some Extent	4. To a Great Extent	5. To a Very Great Extent
	Cadbury Enterprises **Team Team Meeting** **Effectiveness Survey**					
19.	To what extent do your *CETeam* members take proper action on assigned follow-up activities?	1	2	3	4	5
20.	Overall, to what extent are you satisfied with your *CETeam* accomplishments to date?	1	2	3	4	5
21.	Overall, to what extent are you satisfied with your *CETeam* leader?	1	2	3	4	5
22.	Overall, to what extent are you satisfied with your *CETeam* members?	1	2	3	4	5
	Please answer the following questions if your CETeam is using an assigned facilitator:					
23.	To what extent has the role of your *CETeam* facilitator been made clear to you?	1	2	3	4	5
24.	To what extent has your facilitator been helpful to your *CETeam*?	1	2	3	4	5

Written Comments

In the space below, please provide any comments you wish to make regarding how the *CETeam* meeting process could be improved at Cadbury Enterprises.

Thank you for your participation in this survey.

Section 4

Survey Support Materials

To assist you in your survey efforts, this section provides additional examples or tools. Electronic copies of these letters and forms are also included on the accompanying CD-ROM for your use in creating your own documents:

- A sample letter to survey participants.

- Sample mail-in survey instructions.

- A blank survey questionnaire page that you may copy and use to create your own survey instrument. Should you wish to use other scales or response options, you can easily create your own instrument using any word processing software.

- Sample survey code lists and coding sheets, which you can use as examples to create your own code structure and create the coding for your survey.

- Resources for designing and processing your survey and analyzing your survey results.

SAMPLE SURVEY ANNOUNCEMENT LETTER

Please note: This letter may be modified to describe any kind of proposed survey effort.

July 10, 2005

TO: All Cadbury Enterprises Members

FROM: Dan Jones, President

Our organization is continually searching for ways to improve through increased employee involvement. We are currently considering the implementation of a team approach to our Quality Improvement Process, as was described in our recent newsletter. To help us assess the readiness of our organization to undertake a team approach, we have decided to conduct a survey, and we are asking you to participate.

The survey is completely anonymous. There will be no names placed on the survey answer sheets. Instead, you will be assigned a code number to be used for grouping responses. A total summary of answers from across the organization will be created and shared with you.

I consider this to be an important opportunity for our organization. Therefore, I am requesting that you take part in the survey, to be conducted on July 20, 2005.

I wish to express my appreciation for your cooperation in this task.

MAIL-IN SURVEY ANNOUNCEMENT LETTER

July 10, 2005

Memo to: Mail-In Survey Respondents
            Field Sales Employees

From: Mark Thomas
            Organization Development Group

All field sales employees of Cadbury Enterprises are being asked to respond to the enclosed Team Readiness Survey. This survey has been designed to gather information about the readiness of our organization to undertake a team approach to our Quality Improvement efforts.

The information that you provide will be combined with that of the other field sales survey respondents and summarized in a report for all field sales employees.

Using the enclosed preaddressed envelope, send the completed answer sheets directly to the Organization Development Group. They will tabulate all results and provide management with an analysis of the combined data.

You will receive feedback from management about the results of the survey within the next two months.

On the enclosed answer sheet, you will note a box containing a work group code number. This number, assigned by the Organization Development Group and used by all field sales members, allows responses to be combined in a summary report.

Please read carefully the instructions on the questionnaire booklet and on the answer sheet. Where you see the word "organization," think of Cadbury Enterprises; for "supervisor," think of the person to whom you directly report.

So that we can properly process your survey results, please return your answer sheet and questionnaire booklet to the Organization Development Group in the enclosed envelope by July 20.

If you have any questions, please feel free to contact me at extension 3235. Thank you for your cooperation.

5. To a Very Great Extent

4. To a Great Extent

3. To Some Extent

2. To a Little Extent

1. To a Very Little Extent

CADBURY ENTERPRISES

Sample Survey Code List

SUP/NON-SUP
DEPARTMENT CODE
X X X X | X X

Department Codes (First Four Digits)

Hourly		Salaried	
1100	Yard/Nursery	5000	Forestry
1200	Woodroom/Pulpmill	5100	Power/Engineering/Maintenance
1300	Beater room	5200	Industrial relations
1400	Paper machines	5300	Public affairs/Training
1500	Coaters	5400	Purchasing
1600	Supercalenders	5500	Accounting
1700	Finishing room	5600	Computer services
1800	Quality control	5700	Administrative
1900	Technical services	5800	Production
2000	Power plant	5900	Research/QC/Technical services
2100	Storeroom	6000	Marketing/Sales/Distribution
2200	Utility		
2300	Watchman		
2400	Maintenance		

Supervisory/Non-Supervisory (Last Two Digits)

10   Non-Supervisory
20   Supervisors

Examples

A non-supervisory employee in the Beater room:

1 3 0 0 1 0

A supervisor in Purchasing:

5 4 0 0 2 0

SURVEY CODE SHEET

The ability to analyze the Cadbury Enterprises Survey results is directly affected by the accuracy of the survey code used by each participant. You will note that on the upper right-hand portion of the Survey Answer Sheet there is provision for a six-digit *Work Group Code Number*. This number is used to sort the survey responses into meaningful categories. This six-digit code represents the following:

Area of work	Department number			Position	Mgt. level
⇓	⇓	⇓	⇓	⇓	⇓
X	X	X	X	X	X

From the list below, please select the code numbers that correspond to your department, functional area of assignment and related duties, and position level and *enter the code numbers in the appropriate boxes on the answer sheet.*

Digit 1—Your *Area of Work*:

1	Administration
2	Clinical
3	Pre-clinical
4	Technical development
5	Regulatory

Digits 2, 3, 4—Your *Department Number*:

X	X	X	Enter the three-digit number for your department. If you are unsure of the number, please contact the secretary for your department.

Digit 5—Your *Position*:

1	Grades 71 through 76 or 24 through 29
2	Grades 1 through 5
3	Grades 6 and 7
4	Grades 8 and 9
5	Grades 10 through 12
6	Grades 13 through 18

Digit 6—Your *Management Level* (If you are *not* a manager, please enter a "1"):

1	Not a manager
2	Grades 3 through 7
3	Grades 8 and 9
4	Grades 10 through 12
5	Grades 13 through 18

Examples of completed Work Group Code Numbers are as follows:

Manager, Human Resources

1	9	2	8	4	3
⇓		⇓		⇓	⇓
Administration		Human resources		Grade 8	Management levels 8 and 9

Administrative Assistant, Pre-clinical

3	8	0	8	1	1
⇓		⇓		⇓	⇓
Pre-clinical		Chemistry		Grade 73	Not a manager

Director, Clinical Research

2	9	9	3	5	4
⇓		⇓		⇓	⇓
Clinical		Cardiovascular		Grade 10	Management levels 10–12

Once you have filled in the work group code number on the survey answer sheet, please fill in the corresponding numbered circle below each box. An example of a completed work group code number is illustrated on the upper left-hand side of the answer sheet.

If you have any questions about coding your survey answer sheet, please contact Dianna Jones at extension 6875.

OTHER SURVEY RESOURCES

There are many books that offer useful advice on all aspects of the survey process. In addition, there are several software programs with widely varying features, capabilities, and cost that you can use to process and analyze survey data (some software programs have survey design capability as well). There is also a wealth of information available through various Web sites, and some of these are also listed. Because Web sites are being added at an astonishing rate, this list is by no means complete.

Books

Bauer, Robert W., and Sandra S. Bauer. 2003. *The Question Book.* Amherst, MA: HRD Press.

———. 2002. *The Question Book Goes Interactive.* Amherst, MA: HRD Press.

Church, Allan H., and Janine Waciawski. 1998. *Designing and Using Organizational Surveys.* Hampshire, UK: Gower Publishing.

Denison, Daniel R. 1997. *Corporate Culture and Organizational Effectiveness.* Hoboken, NJ: John Wiley & Sons.

Dillman, Don A. 1999. *Mail and Internet Surveys: The Tailored Design Method.* Hoboken, NJ: John Wiley & Sons.

Edwards, Jack E. 1996. *How to Conduct Organizational Surveys: A Step-by-Step Guide.* Thousand Oaks, CA: Sage Publications.

Edwards, Mark R., and Ann J. Ewen. 1996. *360 Degree Feedback: The Powerful New Model for Employee Assessment and Performance Improvement.* New York: AMACOM.

Fink, Arlene, Ed., and Mark S. Litwin. 1995. *The Survey Kit: How to Analyze Survey Data / How to Measure Survey Reliability and Validity / How to Sample in Surveys / How to Design Surveys / How to Report Survey Results.* Thousand Oaks, CA: Sage Publications.

Fink, Arlene, and Jacqueline B. Kosecoff. 1998. *How to Conduct Surveys: A Step by Step Guide.* Thousand Oaks, CA: Sage Publications.

Folkman, Joe. 1998. *Making Feedback Work: Turning Feedback from Employee Surveys into Change.* Provo, UT: Executive Excellence.

Folkman, Joe, and Jack Zenger. 1996. *Employee Surveys That Make a Difference: Using Customized Feedback Tools to Transform Your Organization.* Provo, UT: Executive Excellence.

Howard, Ann. 1994. *Diagnosis for Organizational Change: Methods and Models (The Professional Practice).* New York: Guilford Press.

Kraut, Allen I., Ed. 1996. *Organizational Surveys: Tools for Assessment and Change (Social and Behavioral Science Series).* San Francisco, CA: Jossey-Bass.

Lehtonen, Risto, and Erkki Pahkinen. 2004. *Practical Methods for Design and Analysis of Complex Surveys.* Hoboken, NJ: John Wiley & Sons.

Lepsinger, Richard, and Anntoinette D. Lucia. 1997. *The Art and Science of 360 Degree Feedback.* San Francisco, CA: Jossey-Bass.

Rea, Louis M., and Richard A. Parker. 1997. *Designing and Conducting Survey Research*. San Francisco, CA: Jossey-Bass.

Salant, Patricia, and Don A. Dillman. 1994. *How to Conduct Your Own Survey*. Hoboken, NJ: John Wiley & Sons.

Spunt, Trevor M. 1999. *Guide to Customer Surveys: Sample Questionnaires and Detailed Guidelines for Creating Effective Surveys*. New York: The Customer Service Group.

Tornow, Walter W., Ed. 1998. *Maximizing the Value of 360 Degree Feedback: A Process for Successful Individual and Organizational Development*. San Francisco, CA: Jossey-Bass.

Walonick, David S. 1997. *Survival Statistics*. Bloomington, MN: StatPac.

Westgaard, Odin. 1999. *Tests That Work: Designing and Delivering Fair and Practical Measurement Tools That Work*. San Francisco, CA: Jossey-Bass.

Survey Processing and Statistical Analysis Assistance and Software

Apian Software. SurveyPro 2.0 survey design, processing, and analysis software. SurveyHost web survey hosting software. 800-237-4565; sales@apian.com.

Bauer & Associates. Comprehensive support in survey design, administration, analysis, processing, and feedback of survey results. 810-231-0400; bauersurvy@aol.com.

Saja Software. Survey Select Expert Software for survey design, processing, and analysis. 800-945-0040; info@surveyselect.com.

StatPac. StatPac survey processing and statistical analysis software. 612-925-0159; statbook-sales@statpac.com.

SPSS. A wide array of survey data entry, data preparation, statistical analysis, and reporting software and support services. 800-543-2185; sales@spss.com.

Survey Crafter. Survey Crafter Professional 2.7 for survey creation, editing, analysis, and reporting. 877-650-8527; info@surveycrafter.com.

Web Sites

Apian Software: www.apian.com

Bauer & Associates: www.bauerandassociates.com

Golden Hills Software: www.surveygold.com

MarketTools: www.zoomerang.com

SPSS: www.spss.com

StatPac: www.statpac.com

Survey Crafter: www.surveycrafter.com

SurveyZ: www.surveyz.com

Section 5

Team Effectiveness
CD-ROM Toolkit Instructions

T*he Team Effectiveness CD-ROM Toolkit* is included with this book. The CD is a filing cabinet of files that were used to create the information in the book. There are no software programs on the CD—it is only an electronic storage device, similar to backup CDs that you would normally create to protect your data.

To use the CD, simply go to your CD drive (either through My Computer or Windows Explorer) and double-click on TESW CD.

The CD contains the following folders:

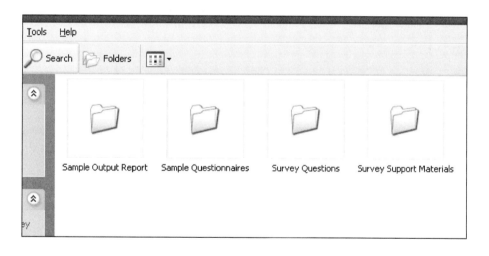

Select the folder you want and double-click on it. For example, if you want to view/use one of the sample questionnaires, double-click on the Sample Questionnaires folder and the following will appear on your screen:

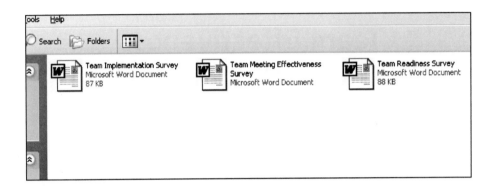

Double-click on the sample survey you want to view/use and the survey you have selected will open in Microsoft Word.

You may use any of the files contained on the CD to meet your individual survey needs. Obviously, they will need to be modified to meet your requirements, but this can be easily accomplished if you are reasonably familiar with Microsoft Word.

Index